D0870480

Homemade
Character

Replacing the Missing Ingredients

Doug Newton

Homemade Character
© 2010 by Douglas Newton

Published by Mary's Place Publishing
a division of Mary's Place, Inc.
Mailing Address:
1302 Lake Shore Dr.
Greenville, IL 62246

Printed in the United States of America

ISBN 0-9748257-2-7

For information about all releases from Mary's Place Publishing visit our website at www.marysplace.org.

To Howard and Jeannette Newton
who never stopped loving me
in spite of the fact that
they couldn't have imagined
what would come out of the oven
when I was born—and sometimes
worried that I had
a few missing ingredients!

Contents

Foreword

I began writing this book when I was 38 years old. I'm now 55. Seventeen years have gone by! You'd think I'd have more to show for it than 154 pages. There are novelists who crank out more pages than that in two months.

What took me so long? I suppose in a book on character I shouldn't make excuses. Let's just say, there's been a lot going on.

Nevertheless, it's done now. And I can see some benefits in the long, slow process. Over the years, as I connected, disconnected and reconnected time and time again with the mission of this book, I found my passion for it resurging every time.

But I remember saying to my wife several times over the years, "I've missed the big wave of interest in character development. Everyone's writing about it. This topic will be passé."

Then two years... three years... five years ticked by, and I'd begin to notice the silence. *No one's talking about shaping character.* I'd see more disconcerting evidence of the cultural decline of moral virtues.

So I'd find some little blocks of time to eke out a few more paragraphs of insights and advice with a refreshed sense of missionary zeal.

Another benefit of a seventeen-year project is the opportunity it affords me to triple-check many of the assertions and recommendations in this book. Our kids—the guinea pigs for testing these nonscientific theories—were 13 and 11 when I started writing. Today they are adults with homes and careers, and provide some credible evidence that my wife's and my shared convictions and practices were constructive, not destructive. They were good kids, but are even better adults. Something seems to have worked.

The evidence goes beyond our own kids, however.

Over the course of 17 years I have spent five years administrating a team of excellent educators in a boarding school for many teens who needed remedial character development as a result of broken lives and homes. There, these convictions were further shaped and systematized in the form of policies and procedures. Scores of teens were successfully reshaped into people of moral virtue.

During the remaining 12 of 17 years I have edited a nationwide magazine which puts me in touch with a host of gifted authors who write as informal experts on everyday family life. Plus, I have spoken annually to thousands of people at churches, camps, retreats, colleges and writers conferences where my ideas received the honing that honest feedback affords.

Finally, for many of the 17 years I served as a pastor to congregations from 30 people (in an impoverished downtown church) to 800 people (in a bustling small college town) where I currently pastor. In such a role as observer, counselor and confessor, I have become even more convinced that the "old ways" this book applauds deserve to be rediscovered in our ultramodern, techno-shaped lives.

However, as committed as I am to the message of this book, I simply offer it to the reader in the "for whatever it's worth" category. It is definitely not the final word coming from a final authority.

I know who the Final Authority is. And while I have intentionally kept religious and biblical allusions in this book to a minimum, not wanting to imply that good character can only be shaped in "good Christians," here is the place I am pleased to state my love for God, my lifelong commitment to follow His Son, Jesus Christ, and my absolute need of His Holy Spirit as my Enabler.

If any human being can ever acquire any moral virtue, it is only because our Creator has invited us and designed us to be like Him—if not now—then one day by His grace.

We have His Word on that.

Chapter One

Chocolate Chips Cookies

I love chocolate chip cookies. With pecans. This is a character flaw worth having. So to begin this book on character development my mind naturally drifts toward an analogy that involves those rich, gooey confections.

I long for fresh-out-of-the-oven chocolate chip cookies like the faithful await the Second Coming. Only once or twice in our years of marriage has my wife, an expert baker, failed to bake a superb batch of chocolate chip cookies. But it has happened.

One time the cookies came out of the oven flat. *Something went terribly wrong!* Shock waves rocked the household of faith. Torturous minutes ticked by as we waited for them to cool. *What would they taste like?*

We gathered around the cookie sheet like mourners before an open casket and prepared ourselves for the loss of the "long-delayed, always expected something that we live for." (My apologies to Tennessee Williams who did not intend his wonderful line from the *Glass Menagerie* to be applied to chocolate chip cookies!)

We couldn't wait any longer. We had to know! *Had it all been a waste? Were we to face tragedy? Why us, Lord?* I picked up a hot limp cookie and let one bite sag from my fingers into my mouth. Hot! Hot! Too hot! I sucked in air vainly attempting to vanquish the heat that had already scalded my tongue. But even through the pain of seared taste buds the truth was sadly clear. Something went terribly, terribly wrong!

All heads turned toward my wife. The unspoken words *How? How could this happen?* dripped like tears from our eyes. Crushed and despairing, she collapsed in my arms begging for forgiveness...

Okay, so it wasn't exactly like that. But a couple of times the cookies didn't turn out tasting very good. Here's my point.

When you have a cookie recipe that produces wonderful chocolate chip cookies every time, and one day the cookies turn out poorly, what do you do? Do you throw away the recipe and frantically look for a new one in the dog-eared back issues of *Better Homes and Garden*? Of course not. You simply retrace your baking steps to discover the missing ingredient. Then you make a new batch, being more careful to include that missing ingredient.

What does this have to do with character development? It is an analogy that gets at the heart of the basic argument of this book. *Our culture used to turn out people with better character. If that is no longer occurring, there must be some missing ingredients. Identify those missing ingredients. Put them back into the cultural mix, if possible. And out come people of character again.*

Some people may argue—indeed they have tried—that our nostalgia about the "good old days" distorts the facts and that people are no worse today than they were a hundred years ago. Others charge that what we call character is the product of a male-dominated western European mindset, and the traits once valued but no longer prevalent—like courage—are not worth a breath of aspiration.

It is not the scope of this book to debate that point, even though we could marshal chapter upon chapter of evidence of a precipitous decline in moral character in the last 40 years, tracked and quantified, for example, by the well-known *Index of Leading Cultural Indicators*. That decline has been summarized by such cultural commentators as William Bennett and James Q. Wilson.

Perhaps more than anything else, America's cultural decline is evidence of a shift in the public's attitudes and beliefs. Social scientist James Q. Wilson writes that "the powers exercised by

the institutions of social control have been con-
strained and people, especially young people, have
embraced an ethos that values self-expression over
self-control." ...Our society now places less value
than before on what we owe to others as a matter of
moral obligation; less value on sacrifice as a moral
good; less value on social conformity and respect-
ability; and less value on correctness and restraint
in matters of physical pleasure and sexuality.

Bill Bennett
Wall Street Journal, May 13, 1993

The main premise of this book is that missing in-gredients, which have led to this documented decline, can be identified and reintroduced into the cultural mix.

This is the crux of the matter. There once was a way of life, now nearly extinct, that tended to foster the development of character traits in young people. Traits like courage, honesty, respect, diligence, perseverance and gratitude were prized and promoted in the context of home and public life. Moral character was, in fact, homemade—like my wife's chocolate chip cookies.

Unfortunately, the patterns of home and public life have changed so drastically in the last half-century, that we have passed a point of no return for restoring those social patterns widely. The traditional family unit and its accompanying "home-oriented" lifestyle, largely responsible for teaching the language of character in our homes, neighborhoods, churches and schools, will probably never be able to re-gain its status as the premier model for family life.

So how can the missing ingredients in the recipe for character development ever be reintroduced, even if they can be rediscovered? This is precisely the question addressed by this book. But before we jump into the "how" we must come to terms with what we mean by character.

> Traits like courage, honesty, respect, diligence, perseverance and gratitude were prized and promoted in the context of home and public life.

Character as Habits of Behavior

Character is not something we have in the way that a person "has" red hair or a quick wit. Nor is character something that describes who we are, as if we could call ourselves "courageous" in the same way we call a person "handsome."

Instead, character is related to what we do consistently. It relates to "habits of behavior." It is true that we often refer to people as *courageous* or *respectful*. But that is not because they have acquired some trait, like a person acquires a good tan.

We call people *courageous* when we observe their lives and discover that they consistently do things that others would shy away from. We call people *respectful* when we notice how often they act thoughtfully when others would be blunt and pushy.

The Greek philosopher Aristotle explained it this way:

> *Moral virtues come from habit... They are in us neither by nature, nor in despite of nature, but we are furnished by nature with a capacity for receiving them, and we develop them through habit... These virtues we acquire by first exercising them, as in the case of the other arts. Whatever we learn to do, we learn by actually doing it: men come to be builders, for instance, by building, and harp players by playing the harp.*
>
> Nichomachean Ethics, *Book II, Section 1*

Since character is nothing more than habits of behavior associated with people who behave consistently in a certain manner, then we can ask this question: What social and cultural ingredients once produced those habits? And how can we introduce those ingredients into a contemporary culture that has strayed so far from the old recipe?

Each of the following chapters keys off of an "icon" or image from by-gone days that represents an ingredient of character development that is currently missing. We will look at each missing ingredient in some detail and reveal basic strategies for inserting those ingredients back into the cultural mix. These icons and the character trait or element each one represents are as follows:

Chores... *Responsibility*
Castor Oil... *Pain*
Woodshed... *Consequences*
Ma'am... *Respect*
Black and White TV... *Simplicity*
Cold Peas... *Gratitude*
Hand-Me-Downs... *Resourcefulness*
Table Talk... *Accountability*
Helping Dad... *Excellence*
Vick's Vaporub... *Acceptance*

At the end of each chapter I offer a recipe for replacement that summarizes and applies the lessons learned.

Underlying the entire program is the assumption that these strategies must be employed in relatively small groupings of people. We cannot recreate a culture of character by addressing the problem globally or nationally.

Instead small groups of people who are bound together into cohesive units comprise little "worlds" of their own—worlds with a more malleable culture and ethos. These little cultures—the culture of the classroom, youth group, church congregation, college campus and, especially, family—can be recreated. People in those mini-cultures can be taught to speak and live out the language of character.

It would be nice if the whole world baked chocolate chip cookies like my wife's. But that not being the case, at least I can work in that delicious direction by passing on the recipe one house at a time.

Chapter Two

Chores

I grew up (some may question that) at a home with about two acres of lawn and enough trees to keep the world stocked with toilet paper for a couple of centuries even if Montezuma's Revenge struck worldwide… the entire time. Fortunately that home was in upstate New York where the snow melts and green grass grows only long after spring has sprung in most of America weeks before. So my banishment to the Island of Lawn Care was shorter than the poor children in the steamy South who barely had time for an iced tea break before the lawn needed mowing again.

But then there were those maple trees in our yard. Funny how I never saw the beauty in the maple reds and yellows every autumn like those adults who bought leaf rakes but never had to use them themselves as long as they had three boys whom they could conscript for the meager sum of fifty cents per week allowance. Funny how I can't appreciate the vivid hues of autumn without hearing a metally, scraping sound in my mind. Funny how vernal green buds remind me less of the wonder of rebirth than the horror of what those buds will become—burgundy hoards of barbarian leaves descending from the upper territories to conquer my summer vacation.

Raking leaves was hard work, and it never seemed to end. "Why can't we just wait until all the leaves fall and only have to rake them once?" was a reasonable proposal I offered - once.

"Because they will kill the grass if they sit there too long," Dad replied coldly as he put the rake back in my hands.

"Exactly. That'll solve both of my problems." Impeccable logic notwithstanding, I raked leaves three or four times a season, praying, pleading for the hard cold rains of November to come in September and strip the trees bare in one great blow.

God never heard my prayer. And so I raked and raked and raked. To this day, I am very good at any repetitious motion involving back and forth movements. Raking leaves. Shoveling snow. Preaching too enthusiastically.

These repetitious activities that I grew up doing were called **chores**. If you are reading this book and are under the age of eighteen, perhaps you should try sounding out this unfamiliar word. Look it up in the dictionary. I'll wait for you to get back. You might have to use the *Oxford English Dictionary*. It defines lots of words that have passed out of contemporary usage.

Chores are a missing ingredient in our culture. I saw this first hand during my years administrating a boarding school in eastern Kentucky. Numerous times the following scenario played out with nearly every new high school student who experienced sweat for the first time.

"What is dripping from my body!" the horror-stricken teen shrieks after the first two minutes on dish crew.

"That's sweat, Marty," informs the supervising staff member.

"Why is it dripping from my body?"

"Because it's ninety degrees Fahrenheit and ninety percent humidity. It's August, you're in Kentucky, and you're standing over a sink filled with steaming hot water in a kitchen that resembles a walk-in oven. That's why."

"I wanna leave."

"Of course," the seasoned staff member acknowledges the plaintive cry he's heard hundreds of times before. "But right now it's time to do dishes."

The other students, the ones who had been doing hard time for years, have wry smiles of recognition wrinkling their faces as they listen out of the corner of their ears.

"But I don't do dishes," counters Marty, as matter-of-factly as if giving his eye color to a licensing clerk at the state motor vehicle bureau.

"I understand that, Marty. That's partly why you've found your way to our school. Be brave. It was for such a time as this that you have come."

Marty's eyes were vacant and despairing. The staff member's light-hearted biblical allusion was lost on this teen-in-anguish.

"Just go ahead and start washing the plates."

Marty eyes the stack of plates reaching to the ceiling. Within three seconds he goes through several of Kuebler-Ross' stages of grief:

(*Disbelief*) "I can't believe you expect me to..."

(*Denial*) "This can't be happening to me."

(*Anger*) "How dare you bring me...!"

"Marty, put your hands in the water. We'll work together."

"But you don't understand. I don't do dishes," he whines.

With unassailable patience born of vast experience and the prospect of telling another "good one" to his wife, the unflappable staff member reaches out to take Marty's hands (*touch therapy*), gently moves them into the water, and makes the long-delayed introduction, "Marty, this is dishwater. Dishwater, this is Marty."

During the 1990s we had students come to us from

all across America, from urban homes and rural homes, from rich homes and poor homes, from broken homes and *Ozzie and Harriet* homes. Almost all of these students shared one common trait. They did not have to take out the trash, mow the lawn, do the dishes, pick up their rooms, help fix dinner or sort and fold laundry. We even had students whose

> **Chores are a thing of the past for most young people, an affliction like polio that no longer poses a threat to their freedom of movement.**

parents offered money (in one case $100!) to get them to pick up their room.

Some people may say, "Well, that may be the way kids are who came to your boarding school."

Excuse me, but these were not dysfunctional kids. Not in the least. Every single one of them was video game literate!

Accept the fact. Chores are a thing of the past for most young people, an affliction like polio that no longer poses a threat to their freedom of movement. But chores are an ingredient that cannot be excluded from the recipe of character development. Ways must be found to bring chores back into our mini-cultures.

First we must understand the nature of a true chore as opposed to mere "busy work" which does not promote character development effectively.

The big difference between a chore and busy work

has to do with the meaning of the work. Both can be monotonous. Both can be repetitious. But busy work has little meaning. In contrast a true chore will be meaningful in three ways.

A Sense of Contribution

In the bygone days of chores, young people were "forced" to work before and after school. The cows had to be milked. If school started at eight o'clock, the cows came first at six. There were stalls to be cleaned, fences to be painted, clothes to be taken off the line, rugs to be beaten, weeds to be pulled and a host of other jobs that also "came first." It was unthinkable to play before the chores were done.

Were children back then different than they are now? Were they once enthused about folding laundry? "Oh mother dearest, may I fold the laundry? Oh may I, please, may I?" Unlikely.

Children have always enjoyed wandering, exploring, imagining and playing instead of working. And yet fifty years ago not only did children put first things first with the prodding "encouragement" of their parents, but they did it with little complaint. How did this happen?

Certainly many factors contributed. It was a societal norm, so a kid didn't feel like a freak when he couldn't come out and play until his chores were done.

Mercifully bereft of television, children were not

taught the language of "back talk" that so easily wears a parent down to the point of letting the kid off rather than listening to the incessant arguments.

But most importantly, the required chores were part of a meaningful whole that made the home function.

Chores were often necessary for the survival and well-being of the family. If the cows weren't milked, there would be serious impact on the family's livelihood. If wood wasn't gathered in, the house would be cold in the winter. The work may not have been fun or a kid's first choice, but there was a sense that it really counted.

> Any chore—to be a worthwhile chore— must give a sense that real loss will be suffered or real problems will result "If I don't do my part."

Today the welfare of the family rarely hangs in the balance over chores getting done. If the worse that can happen for failing to do a chore is that "I might get yelled at" or "so my room's a little messy" then there will be no sense of contributing to the common good.

Any chore—to be a worthwhile chore—must give a sense that real loss will be suffered or real problems will result "if I don't do my part." That does not mean that all chores will seem important in and of themselves. In the days before vacuum cleaners, hanging a nearly-threadbare braided rug over a clothesline and beating it two hundred times with a flat paddle did not seem important to the person wielding the paddle and choking on the dust. But good health and cleanliness went hand in hand and were considered very important. That meant attacking dust, not letting it take over. Beating rugs was a strategic battle in waging this ongoing war. Children were often moved up to the front lines in the campaign to defeat dirt. Theirs was a significant role.

During World War II millions of adults and children put up with hardship and inconvenience, inspired by a sense of contributing to the war effort. They accepted the rationing of everything from gas to sugar. They invested in war bonds. Residents in coastal cities doused their lights at sundown and pulled the blanket of darkness over themselves to keep from being a target for bombs should the enemy ever try to bring the war across the ocean. They went to work in ammunition and textile factories. They accepted these unpleasant conditions because, "it is something I can do to help."

That's what a chore must be. It must leave a young person with a sense of contributing to the common good. People who have a hard time getting Johnny to "do anything around the house" need to give Johnny something that counts. Even though he may be only eight years old, he can keep track of the oil change schedule for the family cars, for example. Give Johnny something more important to do than just making his bed, something that will benefit the family, and making his bed will most likely get done, too.

A Sense of Competence and Trustworthiness

I remember what it was like to graduate from a push mower to a riding mower. My Dad never said it in so many words, but by handing me the keys that first time I knew he was moving me up to a new level of trust.

I was being trusted not to "hotrod around" on a dangerous machine, not to crush the waves of blossoms that splashed from the flower beds against the shoreline of the green lawn, and not to run aground against the gnarled maple tree roots that lay submerged like coral reefs beneath the surface of the grass. I was being trusted not to grind over top of the fallen branches and not to point the mower toward the neighbors' windows or cars coming along Fyler Road. For one whole mowing season I actually wanted to mow. I enjoyed a rite of passage reflected in my "promotion."

> **Chores must be designed in such a way that a person can graduate to higher levels of competence and trust.**

To avoid the trap of busy work, chores must be designed in such a way that a person can graduate to higher levels of competence and trust. True chores that build character are gradual initiations into adult responsibilities. Too often adults fail in this important aspect, because

17

they are afraid to "turn over the keys" to someone who may make serious mistakes.

But stop and think about this. The only way to teach a young person to drive is to let her take complete control of a multi-thousand dollar vehicle that causes billions of dollars of damage annually—before she even knows where the turn signals are located! (Driver Ed. teachers should get hazard pay!)

There is no way around this educational method of letting her operate the car before she really knows how. But we fail to apply this principle in other situations.

Chores must be based on this general rule: *Give children responsibilities that are beyond their current abilities.* That is what they are eager for. They can't wait to drive, to have their own checkbook or to paint their own room. For children to mature, adults must risk crumpled fenders, bounced checks and splattered carpets.

As children are allowed into these exclusive adult-only competency clubs, they can be inspired by the greater levels of trust to assume greater levels of responsibility. Chores should be seen as schools with opportunities for advancement. Don't just have children clean their rooms or take out the trash or fold the clothes without offering the hope of being given more desirable responsibilities as they prove themselves faithful in the small things.

Let them look forward to being able to stay home by themselves, plan the family vacation or have an after school job. The important thing is to connect the opportunity for advancement to the responsible fulfillment of current chores.

A Sense of Completion

Chores are the things we do every day, things that have to get done even when we would rather be doing something else. They force us to learn the habit of thinking long-term. *If I don't keep up on my room, mold may grow under my bed!*

Chores are vital to character development precisely because they are so routine and repetitious. But that leads to a problem of feeling like nothing is being accomplished, nothing is getting "done." What is being accomplished by doing dishes day after day, or cleaning the bathroom, or making your bed? Things just get messed up again. That's why chores, even meaningful ones, can begin to seem like mere busy work.

So there's one more characteristic of a true chore. It must be set into a context of accomplishment. Since chore work often yields no visible progress, there must be a sense that something is getting done. How do you create that sense? By verbalizing what the chores accomplish.

Example A: *"When you put your clothes in the hamper, you save me at least ten minutes of work gathering up dirty clothes."*

Example B: *"When you help dry dishes, I don't feel*

like I am all by myself. I enjoy your company."

Example C: *"When you mow the lawn you help us set a good example for our neighbors of taking care of property."*

These are not accomplishments that our culture rewards, like academic excellence or sports achievements. But their significance can be verbalized to young people. Giving the gift of extra time to a busy person *(example A)*, making a person feel supported *(example B)*, and exemplifying good citizenship and stewardship *(example C)* are accomplishments more valuable than any trophy can signify.

However, young people will not see these accomplishments easily. Adults must intentionally verbalize them regularly.

If character is the result of habitual behavior, then nothing spells habit like c-h-o-r-e. But as important as chores are to character development, we must now turn our attention to the next missing ingredient. The lack of this ingredient results in the greatest obstacle to fulfilling chores and building character.

ℛ*ECIPE* 𝒮*TEPS: CHORES*

◨ Find work that contributes to the common good.

◨ Make chores a top priority.

◨ Give adult-level responsibilities.

◨ Create opportunities for graduating to higher levels of trust and competence.

◨ Don't be deterred by belly-aching.

- *Don't feel cruel and guilt-ridden.*
- *Don't let up on fair expectations.*
- *Don't get tired of the struggle to "insist."*
- *Don't bribe.*

◨ Verbalize the value of what's being accomplished.

Chapter Three

Castor Oil

Pain and I became friends during the years I played goalie in a sport called lacrosse. Lacrosse, an old American Indian game, is very popular in the Northeast and Mid-Atlantic states. I grew up in Syracuse with a rich winning tradition in lacrosse, so it was an elite sport at my high school. The competition for starting positions was tough.

I loved playing goalie, being the last hope against defeat, charged with the responsibility of keeping a hard rubber ball (slightly smaller than a baseball) out of a six feet by six feet goal. This is very hard to do, because the ball would be hurled from any direction at speeds exceeding 120 miles an hour.

A good lacrosse goalie, like a hockey goalie, will use anything he can to block the incoming shot—stick, hands, thighs, forearms, chest and face. Of course, goalies are heavily padded from head to foot, so the real pain happens when you have to turn around to retrieve the ball that found its way into the net behind you.

A goalie must be very quick. Sometimes there were so many people blocking my vision, I couldn't even see the offensive attacker fire off a shot. The ball would suddenly appear five feet away rocketing toward the upper corner of the goal. Snap! My oversize lacrosse stick twitched upward to snag the rock hard projectile. I was quick. But of course the ball made it past me enough times so that I longed to be even quicker.

One day the idea struck me, "Maybe if I get rid of all this goalie padding, I will be *motivated* to be even faster."

I was not thrilled by my idea, but it did make some sense. After all, the body's protective reflex action is super fast. The eye can blink incredibly fast to protect itself from the flick of an intruding finger or speck of dirt. This is a totally involuntary action—a reflex action.

"Couldn't I simulate that kind of danger and trigger the much quicker reflex action by not wearing any pads?" I theorized.

So I decided that if greater quickness was the result, I would gladly experiment in practice one day. This I did, and I concluded that there was indeed a real benefit. I seemed to react faster, not to mention the ego-inflating benefit of the awe I received from my dumbfounded teammates.

For the rest of the season I played all my games in just shorts, a T-shirt, padded gloves, a helmet and face shield. I spurned the thigh and arm protectors. Here you may be wondering if, in the interest of good taste, I am not mentioning one very important piece of equipment. No, I didn't even wear one of those. Wow, talk about reflex action kicking in!

But didn't the ball hurt? Yes. Imagine someone doubling up his fist and hitting you with his middle knuckle on the outside of your upper arm. I went home with welts that discolored the next day into perfectly round two-inch purplish bruises.

As the season went on, however, I began to observe something very interesting. The pain seemed to bother me less and less. I still was getting blasted and welted, but the perception of the blow as "painful" decreased.

An Adjustable Pain Threshold?

This lesson has stuck with me, and I take it to be a principle of life: *A person's pain threshold can be raised.* Of course, I never went around teaching it to others. "Here. Let me smack you with my fist over and over for the next two weeks. Trust me. After awhile, it won't seem as painful."

However, I applied this principle to other areas in my own life. I allowed myself to be exposed to pain to inoculate myself against its debilitating effects. That's why I said that pain and I have become friends. I have

25

come to value what it does for me to prepare me for facing life's difficulties.

Many years after my high school lacrosse career, I was sitting in the living room of a 95-year-old woman who as a young girl had traveled to Kentucky in a covered wagon. She had known the suffering of hardscrabble farming in the poor South at the turn of the century. During one of our conversations about the tremendous physical hardships in her life, the topic of her recent cataract surgery came up. I asked her if she had been experiencing any pain.

She replied matter-of-factly, "No, none at all. It hurts a little, but I haven't had any pain."

My mind cocked to one side like a dog's head when it is contemplating a fly on the ceiling. *She said that it hurts a little, but she hasn't felt any pain?*

> **Our culture has been clothing us with more and more padding. What used to be perceived as minor and bearable pain is now perceived as intrusive and unbearable.**

My lacrosse experience came back to me, and I understood. With all her tremendous suffering in life, Mrs. Flora's definition and perception of pain had been so adjusted that a little physical discomfort didn't even qualify for the word "pain."

Now consider this. If the pain threshold can be adjusted upward so that people perceive pain as less

26

and less bothersome, can the pain threshold also be lowered? If a person can grow more impervious to the perception of pain, can one grow more susceptible to the perception of pain? Yes, I think so.

In fact, this is precisely what has happened in our culture. Just the opposite of my lacrosse strategy, our culture has been clothing us with more and more padding. The result is this: *What used to be perceived as minor and bearable pain is now perceived as intrusive and unbearable.*

Pain: Public Enemy Number One

In the past few decades the technological vanguard of our culture has pronounced pain as public enemy number one. An all out war is being waged to rid our lives of any experience of pain. You get the idea that if it were technologically possible, we would accept the removal of all pain from our lives. Our American culture is so intent on padding us against life's hard knocks that we experience it less and less, and become more and more enslaved by the fear of pain.

Consequently, a new unalienable right has forced its way into the classic triumvirate of "life, liberty and the pursuit of happiness." It is the *unalienable right to the absence of pain.* Even our government is being reshaped into an institution charged with the responsibility of protecting its citizens from any pain or discomfort whatsoever.

27

Living pain-free lives is tirelessly promoted and pursued. Headaches, muscle aches and congestion from common colds are facts of life people once accepted. Today they are considered demons that can control us and throw us into wretched behavior unless exorcised by pharmaceutical potions and pills.

It is hard to overestimate the toll on our country exacted by this mindset. It has become the perfect self-justifier. Any commitment can understandably be broken by simply appealing to the "pain defense."

"Your honor, my client should not be held responsible for his actions, because of the pain and discomfort he was experiencing at the time."

The prospect of unwanted pain and suffering excuses the breaking of relationships, the discarding of inconvenient "products of conception" historically known as unborn children, and the disintegration of promises. And the unwanted pain that justifies these moral failures doesn't have to be traumatic in nature.

Considered extremely painful today is the experience, or even just the fear, of "missing out." This is a phantom pain caused by the possibility that a person might not be able to enjoy what he hopes to enjoy.

"Yes, I know I promised that I would take you to the mall, but there is a great game on TV tonight. I'll take you tomorrow night."

The more comfort-oriented we are and the more we become technologically capable of evicting pain from our homes, the softer and weaker all our commitments become. That is to say, the softer and weaker we become.

This is deadly to character formation, because the historically-proven maxim correctly asserts that moral character is produced in the crucible of discomfort, inconvenience and pain. The Bible calls attention to this maxim as well:

> *Not only so, but we also rejoice in our suffering, because we know that suffering produces perseverance; perseverance character; and character, hope.*
>
> *Romans 5:3-4*

Therefore, the removal of pain from our collective cultural life is tantamount to dousing the fires of the crucible.

The Solution

What must be done to address this problem? You can feel it coming can't you. Yes, pain and discomfort must no longer be avoided at all cost. Anyone who is serious about character development must allow pain and discomfort to be a common ingredient in life experiences.

But does that mean we should engage in acts of masochistic machismo ala G. Gordon Liddy's infamous "hand in the candle flame" test of endurance? No, of course not. But we must do two things.

29

We must repudiate our prejudice against pain. Then we must gradually accustom ourselves to pain and practice the art of behaving properly even while experiencing pain. If we should keep our word, then we should keep it even when we have a splitting headache.

Repudiate Our Prejudice

A speech by John F. Kennedy reveals an attitude toward pain and difficulty that seems foreign today, but it needs to be regained by anyone interested in developing character. On the occasion of announcing the United States' commitment to place a man on the moon, Kennedy used this rationale:

"We do these things not because they are easy,
but because they are hard."

He went on to say that taking on difficult challenges "serves to organize the best of our energies and skills."

This attitude of intentionally leaning into the stiff wind of difficulty because it is a "good thing to do" was common sense four decades ago.

Today it sounds like foolishness. *Why would anyone choose anything but the easiest way*, we wonder, conditioned by a computer culture to evaluate things according to user-friendliness. "Always pick the path of least resistance," we counsel, thinking life should always open another check-out line. It goes without saying, "If there is a pill for any ache and pain, you should take it."

Fifty years ago, castor oil was an effective teaching tool if not so effective medicine. It tasted like a concoction of bacon slime and old transmission fluid. Every time that spoonful of liquid bile came toward a young person, one who knew from bitter past experiences what was coming, a rationale was given, "Open up. It'll be good for you." There was nothing wrong with going through a little pain to make oneself better.

It'll be good for you. Were parents meaner back then? Is love and sensitivity an evolutionary development in a new higher order of homo parentis? No. If anything, we are experiencing devolution in this era of guarding little Billy and Sally from anything that makes them feel mad, bad or sad.

The ancient Jurassic parents of fifty years ago used to be able stand up to whining and temper tantrums. They used to be able to say things like:

- *"No. You can't have that now."*
- *"You will have to wait until you save up money."*
- *"I understand that your finger hurts, but you still have to take out the trash."*
- *"I'm sorry your head aches, but there's nothing we can do about it now. Sit still."*
- *"You may not like it, but this is what we are having for dinner tonight."*

Whenever parents said these awfully insensitive

things, they understood that having to suffer the torture of waiting for something was a good thing. Having to go ahead and do normal tasks in spite of a little discomfort was a good thing. Having to sit still—especially when four-year-old Johnny was bored and the preacher was droning on and every itching nerve ending screamed *wriggle!*—was a good thing.

These parents did not run to the medicine cabinet of relief the instant something unpleasant caused their child to cough up a complaint. And horror of horrors, occasionally they would purposely require their children to do something that would create blisters, sore muscles or the forfeiture of playtime – things like putting up hay, or scrubbing windows, or making children walk somewhere instead of chauffeuring them any distance over a half mile.

Parents did not run to the medicine cabinet of relief the instant something unpleasant caused their child to cough up a complaint.

Children were no different than they are today. Those things never struck children as pleasant at the time. But parents knew it was good for them—like castor oil.

If we are ever to regain a culture that produces people of character we must quit running from all pain. We must recognize that it is good for us, and that small spoonfuls of it actually do help us become healthier.

A widely respected doctor renowned for his pioneering work among leprosy victims has written:

> *"My own encounters with pain, though, as well as the specter of painlessness, have produced in me an attitude of wonder and appreciation. I do not desire, and cannot even imagine, a life without pain. For that reason I accept the challenge of trying to restore balance to how we think about pain... Most of us will one day face severe pain. I am convinced that the attitude we cultivate in advance may well determine how suffering will affect us when it does strike."*
>
> Dr. Paul Brand, The Gift of Pain

I join Dr. Brand in that mission. No character development can occur without the presence of pain and discomfort. It is the gravity of the moral world. It is what makes moral choices feel heavy. It is the downward resistance we must push against if we are to get stronger, just as a weight lifter pushes against natural gravity to get physically stronger.

And just as a weight lifter places measured weights on the barbell, young people must be given measured experiences of pain and discomfort.

Enduring Physical Discomfort

Certainly I can't mean it, can I? Don't run to the medicine cabinet for every ache and pain? Yes, I mean it. Bumper stickers in the 60's advocated, *Question Authority.*

I would like to make a modest proposal to change that bumper sticker to *Question Pain Relief.* Every time our society says, "Take a pill for pain relief" we should ask, "Why?"

I am not advocating the dismissal of medicines and medical technology. I am suggesting that we must learn to live with ordinary daily aches and pain without running to pain relievers. But why? By doing so we begin to learn the art of distraction that helps us persist in the presence of pain.

The Principle of Distraction

Do you understand the principle of pain relievers like *Ben Gay*™? They don't actually *relieve* the pain, they just distract the brain's attention away from the deep muscle pain signals.

It works like this. You have had a hard day of washing the windows. Now your back and shoulders ache from the thousands of wiping motions. Your leg muscles are sore from climbing up and down the ladder. The pain you are experiencing is the result of muscle cells tearing apart. Depending on how rapidly you were moving your arms back and forth, you might have gotten your muscles into a state of oxygen debt and experienced a build up of lactic acid which is normally pumped out of your system. But when movements become anaerobic the lactic acids lays in your muscles burning away. Torn cells. Acidic build up. This is why you are in pain.

This is actually a good thing. It is the body's way of telling you to take some time off so that the muscles can rebuild stronger than they were. If you don't heed the warning, you can damage yourself.

When you rub yourself down with *Ben Gay*™, there is no actual relief of what is causing the pain. There is only a change in what your brain is perceiving. Your muscle cells have not miraculously mended. That will take a couple days. The lactic acid has not been pH adjusted and rendered less acidic.

Here is what is happening. A new stimulant is competing for your brain's attention. The chemical properties of the *Ben Gay*™ are stimulating thousands of nerve cells at the surface of the skin. Blood rushes to those aroused cells warming the area where the *Ben Gay*™ is rubbed. These thousands of excited nerve cells are pumping out electrical messages to the brain.

Their route to the brain takes them to the same "gateway" into the brain through which all other signals have to pass from every other part of your body, including those damaged muscle cells from your day's work on the windows. The teeming hoard of signals from the thousands of *Ben Gayed* nerve endings push their way through and drown out the fewer and duller signals from the deeper muscle cells. The result is that the muscle pain seems to go away. It hasn't. It has just momentarily lost this competition for your brain's attention.

To see a similar affect, scratch your left forearm with your finger nail enough to make a mark that hurts a little. Leave it alone for a few seconds. Can you feel it? Now use your right hand to squeeze the back of your neck, like someone is giving you a back rub a little too hard. You will find that while you are squeezing your neck, you don't sense the scratched forearm. Stop squeezing your neck and the pain of the scratched forearm "comes back."

> **If we are to become people who will follow through on our commitments even when we experience some kind of pain, we must learn how to control our reaction to pain.**

Once you recognize that pain is largely a matter of perception you should also be able to realize that there are other, perhaps more valuable, ways to deal with pain. If it is possible for a chemical reaction on the surface of the skin, or a pressure on the back of the neck, to reduce the perception of the "painfulness" of pain, might it not be possible to learn methods of distracting the brain in non chemical ways?

That is the point of allowing ourselves to have to deal with pain. It is not to become macho and impress our friends with feats of fire walking. If we are to become people who will follow through on our commitments even when we experience some kind of pain, we must learn how to control our reaction to pain. We must learn how to perceive pain less painfully. There is no other way of doing this than learning to think of something else more distracting. There are three ways to do this.

The Art of Distraction and the "Greater Problem"

First, I have learned to distract myself from the perception of pain by making myself conscious of a potentially greater problem.

One summer I was visiting my in-laws in upstate New York. They lived just a few hundred feet upstream from a dam that created a small Adirondack lake. Their backyard that bordered the lake was beautiful, framed by a few trees leaning out over the water that seemed to be posing for the camera.

On this occasion, my mother-in-law had been troubled by a few unsightly dead limbs in one of those trees. She wanted them "combed out" for future photos, I suppose. I volunteered to climb up the tree and cut them down.

From the ground it seemed simple. Up in the tree fear gripped me as tightly as I gripped the divided trunk I had to shimmy. It felt like I was fifty feet up dangling over water that was accelerating toward Niagara Falls rather than the Forestport Dam. After repeated starts and stops, huffing and puffing, while sawing away at the largest stubborn branch,

> We must learn how to perceive pain less painfully.

it finally fell and I made it down without drowning.

When I got down, I was amazed at the rush of pain I felt in my arms and legs. Upon closer inspection I found numerous scrapes and bloody cuts from what I then noticed was very rough bark and one-inch prickers on the tree. I was hurting. But I hadn't even noticed the cuts as they were happening. Why? Because the risk of falling from the tree, hitting my head on a branch, and splashing unconscious into the "raging torrent" below me completely occupied my mind. Nothing else could slip in even sideways. The fear of "something worse" happening had reduced my perception of the inflicted pain.

One of the reasons for practicing pain endurance is to learn how to discover those "something worse" things that can happen, and how by keeping the "something worse" in mind, we can endure the pain.

The discipline of daily exercise may often be inconvenient, tiresome or even physically painful when your back aches or head hurts. But every time I walk past an elderly person who is hunched over and tightened up, barely limber enough to step down from a curb,— there's the "something worse"—I remind myself not to give up my workout regimen.

The Art of Distraction and the "Greater Good"

The second aspect in learning the art of distraction is like the first but turned in the opposite direction.

Rather than keeping "something worse" in mind you keep a greater good or desirable goal in view.

I'm embarrassed to say that there have been several times in my adult life that I have told lies. White lies. Black lies. Pick a color. Usually the lie snuck up on me and escaped from my mouth before I even had a chance to trap it. Most of the time it happened when someone was counting on me to get something done and I either forgot altogether, or I had tried but was delayed. I didn't want the person to think he or she was unimportant to me. I hate the thought that he might have even one second of a worry shoot through his mind, "Doug doesn't care."

So out came the lie.

Have you ever noticed how many euphemistic synonyms there are for lying? Prevaricate. Obfuscate. Fudge. Exaggerate. Be disingenuous. Duplicitous. Dishonest. Mendacious. Untruthful. We just hate to call it what it is and admit we lied.

Nevertheless, I have to confess. The last time I lied was about six months before writing this chapter. I was meeting a young father weekly for an hour of casual conversation that was designed by both of us to help him think through some of his personal struggles. Despite his rough, aggressive exterior he was quite insecure. His marriage was chronically rocky. He had never held onto a job for more than a year or two before being fired. Even his parents gave him the cold shoulder.

Somewhere deep inside he knew he was his own worst problem, though he was not fully prepared to own that fact fully. The last thing he needed was to reach out to me and then have me grow tired of him too.

One day I got busy and forgot about our appointment to meet at the burger joint. I didn't even realize I had forgotten until the next night at church when he came walking in and said with searching eyes, "I missed you yesterday."

> **A clear view of achieving some goal of great value can overpower high degrees of pain.**

It's amazing how fast your mind can work when you are motivated to save your skin. It's like reflex action. In the blink of an eye I had already found my rationalization (*It will hurt his feelings if he thinks I plain forgot*), justified myself based on what was better for him (*I can't risk losing his confidence at this point when he is so close to making some important changes*) and even scanned a variety of possible excuses that bore as close a resemblance to truth as possible. The excuse I finally told was 90% true. But still in the end I actually said I had tried to call when I hadn't. I lied.

He accepted my excuse graciously. I walked away. Whew! That was a close one.

Suddenly, I saw myself. In a flash I projected ahead ten to twenty years. I asked myself, *Don't you ever want to become a person who always tells the truth, a person of unquestioned integrity and honesty?*

My answer just as quickly was a resounding yes.

I didn't like the prospect of confessing, especially how that might damage my reputation in his eyes and place an uncomfortable question mark between his trust and me. Nevertheless, at the next possible moment, which meant asking him to delay going into the church meeting, I walked into the pain of self-incrimination and took one more step toward honesty.

A clear view of achieving some goal of great value can overpower high degrees of pain.

The Art of Distraction and the "Significant Other"

Finally, the third aspect of the art of distraction is to find a person you want to please or impress. This technique is one of the few habits of adolescence that actually can be useful in adulthood.

The only difference has to do with whom you choose.

An adolescent chooses to impress in order to win affection or acceptance. So young boys hurtle themselves into acts of silly bravado in hopes of making pretty Suzy swoon. And when they fall and break their head, they bounce back up with a rigid "I'm alright" smile that can last as long as she is watching. Blood and teeth may be falling from their mouth, but the pain will mean nothing as long as she is watching.

The difference from adolescence to adulthood is

that the adult chooses to please and impress those from whom he has nothing to gain. His goal is to be someone pleasing out of admiration for the one he chooses to emulate or honor.

So these days, though I need no greater love and acceptance from my wife than I have already received, I find it easy, even pleasurable, to sweat, to bear all sorts of burdens, to wait patiently, to smile in sickness for her. She is the most important person in the world for whom I want to be and give the best I can.

On a grander scale, though I embrace this in the more abstract way of faith, I am enabled to endure pain as I imagine God's pleasure in me. I do not need and can never hope to deserve His grace. But it is for that very fact that I have the deepest desire to honor Him with personal excellence. *Let all that is within me bless His name.*

As long as we are talking about pain, we might as well get it over with. We need to move on and talk about punishment and consequences in the role of character development. It's time to go out to the woodshed.

$\mathcal{R}$*ECIPE* $\mathcal{S}$*TEPS: CASTOR OIL*

◨ **Raise the pain threshold.**

◨ **Reject the assumption that all pain is bad and should always be avoided.**

◨ **Intentionally practice the art of pain.**

- *Don't always pick the path of least resistance.*

- *Require a period of waiting, even when something could happen immediately.*

- *Don't pursue or offer relief at the very onset of common pain.*

- *Resist the temptation to quit under the weight of discomfort.*

- *Increase moral strength by giving measured experiences of pain and discomfort.*

- *Question pain relief.*

◨ **Learn to control reaction to pain through thinking distracting thoughts.**

- *"If I give in, something worse might happen..."*

- *"If I don't give in, something better can happen..."*

- *"If I press on, someone wonderful will be pleased with me..."*

Chapter Four

Woodshed

Going to the woodshed was as close as a young person could come to meeting his Maker. For that reason and several others, the woodshed was a good place. It was like the Tent of Meeting, the place of atonement. Except unlike Moses and his famous shining face, the only bodily part glowing after an encounter in the woodshed was mercifully covered back up after atonement was made.

In my modern furnace heated home, we needed no woodshed per se. So the woodshed experience moved indoors, like the bathroom had with the advent of indoor plumbing. The woodshed was my parent's bedroom. In all my years of growing up I never did become comfortable being in my parent's bedroom. It always seemed like a holy place, a place where one talked quietly with a broken and contrite spirit. I'm sure it was not my parent's desire for it to be so. And perhaps it wouldn't have become so, had it not been for the numerous times it had to be used as a woodshed. Usually on Sunday afternoons. After church. After a particularly long sermon. After my father had leaned forward casting a lightning bolt gaze in my direction until I paused in my rustling of papers sensing some ominous cloud filling the tabernacle, some haunting presence watching me. My head slowly turned to the left looking down the long pew to see my father's lips mouthing the familiar liturgy, "You're going to get a spanking when you get home."

When we would get home, my Dad, being a liberated and psychology aware father, secured my self esteem before the sentence was carried out by affording me the dignity of choice. "Do you want it *before* or *after* dinner?"

I always chose curtain number one — *before*. My thinking was that the pain of a spanking before dinner made the usual Sunday-after-church Swiss steak dinner seem less distasteful by contrast.

As I grew older and, as I mentioned earlier, began playing sports like lacrosse, the woodshed ceased to be my parents' bedroom. After all, if a hundred mile an hour hard rubber ball could not faze me, my Dad's desk job tender hand was not a significant threat to my nerve endings. At that age, the woodshed became my father's voice. In an instant it could swat me with a tone of disappointment or disapproval that penetrated to a seat of learning far more sensitive than the one once exposed while bending over the edge of the bed.

All those memories are... wonderful! I don't remember the burning sensation, or even the sound of his voice when he used my name disapprovingly, "Douglas!" All I remember now is the security of being held accountable for my actions. Every spanking. Every scolding. Every being sent to my room told me something about me and my mission in life. *Douglas, your choices matter. Make the right ones.*

> **Our culture has become so paranoid about punishment and damaging children that we have left that ingredient out of the cultural mix.**

Yes, punishment must be meted out judiciously. And yes, there are serious abuses in this world physically and emotionally when parents punish children. But there are also lots of car accidents, too. We don't stop driving; we work at driving safely. Neither should we tear down the woodshed.

Our culture has become so paranoid about punishment and damaging children that we have left that ingredient out of the cultural mix. The result is poor character development. But spanking is only one small part of a culture of punishment and accountability, a way of life that taught the importance of human choice. Here are some other woodshed techniques that were commonly employed to "teach young people a lesson" when they made wrong choices.

Require Apologies

When I was eight I stole some matches and accidentally set a neighbor's hay field on fire while showing off to a couple of younger kids. I ran home and put on my best performance of nonchalance and innocence. My mom was in the kitchen as I walked in the door. I didn't know it at the time, but accusation spreads as quickly as fire. My mom had already been on the phone with the neighbors from whom I had stolen the matches and the neighbors whose hay field was now smoldering. That was information she kept from me as she gave me the opportunity to come clean, which of course I didn't.

Fire? At the neighbors? Wow? How'd it happen? My mom's face began to sink and her eyes reddened, I think. I didn't look into them for more than a nanosecond. She presented the evidence of my complicity in the crime. I plea bargained.

There was already a fire there. Some big kids were messing around. I tried to put it out. My mistake was in getting involved. Now she was crying as she pronounced the sentence. She took me by the hand and never let go as we walked—as I was marched—more than a quarter mile down the road to the neighbors where I was forced to face my accusers and say the words "I'm sorry" clearly enough to be heard by one and all.

Those neighbors knew exactly what to do. They did not say, "It's OK. What a fine boy to apologize." They did not see an apology as something that makes things all right and undoes the damage. They stared at me with appropriate disapproval and did not try to make me feel better or less ashamed. They let me live with what I had done. Bravo for them. That was the right thing to do. That is a missing ingredient today: requiring apologies without immediate soothing strokes of forgiveness.

Grant Few Reprieves.

A favorite story of mine involves the Old Testament hero King David. During a time of weakness and evil desire, King David abused his authority and forced a young girl, married to a soldier on military assignment, to have sex with him. She became pregnant, and David tried to cover up his sin by bringing her husband home from military service hoping the couple would have sex. Thus, the pregnancy would appear to be a result of their conjugal visit.

Uriah, her husband, was too honorable to accept the privilege of sexual relations with his wife while his fellow soldiers were still at war. David tried to get him drunk enough to forget his honorable convictions, but those convictions went deeper than the liquor could loosen. Finally, David's solution was to devise Uriah's demise in battle, leaving the beautiful young Bathsheba widowed and available for the king's taking.

As the story unfolds, David is not wracked with guilt and pain over his despicable actions until a prophet named Nathan confronted him and exposed his sins. At that time David saw the sins from God's viewpoint and was stricken with grief. He begged for forgiveness. He apologized in the best possible way, recognizing that his sin was first and foremost an affront to God himself. At that point something happened that teaches a basic lesson about mercy and dealing with bad choices. Nathan, speaking on behalf of God, pronounced David absolutely forgiven. His apology was accepted by God. But...

Forgiveness does not require the removal of consequences.

But! None of the horrible consequences was erased. For the rest of David's life the consequences of his sin were the source of much grief, sorrow and suffering. His family was divided. His wives were sexually assaulted, and he was publicly humiliated. Worst of all, the son born out of David's sin died. This well known story reveals a principle about the woodshed. Forgiveness does not require the removal of consequences.

One of my most painful experiences involved following through on punishing my older daughter even though her attitude toward the punishment was perfect. It happened at Wal-Mart.

Four-year-old Kelcey was told not to touch things

on the shelves. She did. Once again I told her not to do that and gave a brief reason, "You might knock things over." She touched something again. This third time I gave the warning of impending punishment—a spanking "when we get out to the car."

I don't know what got into her, perhaps the mythological song of the sirens beckoning from the shelves was more than she could resist. She steered her hand once again toward the rocky shores and grabbed something. I put it back and pronounced sentence, "You're getting a spanking when we get out to the car." The minutes dragged by for her as we finished our shopping and pushed the cart out to the car. Kelcey had been understandably quiet for the rest of the time in the store.

I opened the car door and used it as a shield and shelter against the marauding social posse who might start screaming, "Child abuse!" I stooped down eye to eye with my four year old convict and rehearsed what was about to happen and why. After I finished my thirty second statement, I asked Kelcey if she had anything to say. That's when my stable world of certainty tilted. She didn't argue like many children might have, pleading and bargaining through tears, "Don't spank me! I won't do it again! Please don't spank me." I could have handled that. But when she said softly, looking straight into my eyes, "Not too hard, Daddy," the scales of justice nearly cracked in two. Here she was saying the best

51

thing she could have possibly said as she laid her life across the palm of my hand and relied on my ability to show mercy through the judicious use of pain.

"Not too hard, Daddy." That was one of the most precious moments of my life, and spanking her that day was like swatting a fly through a roomful of molasses. I could hardly move my hand, but I had to do it. It was the fulfillment of my word. It was the right thing to do. It was the consequence of her choice. And it hurt me more than the thud of a hundred lacrosse balls.

Sometimes the consequences of our choices are not punishments so much as unfulfilled desires. We want to be in shape and feel good about ourselves physically, but we keep caving in to the temptation of chocolate chip cookies and fail to take off the extra pounds we know we should lose. We don't like it, but that's a consequence of our choices. We try to devise technologies that will allow for over indulgence without the consequences. We pay billions for fat free foods. We create a liposuction industry. Even as I write a pill is being perfected that will dissolve fat cells, leaving us free to be thin gluttons.

This is the world we have created for ourselves, one that lets us overspend, overeat, overwork, one that let's us be led into temptation but still delivers us from evil consequences.

This is the world we are passing on to our children. We don't want our children suffering pain. We protect them from the consequences of their choices by giving them second, third and fourth chances to get things right.

Many school systems around the country have grading policies that refuse to let any student get below a "C." They do this to protect the children's self esteem, but it is a joke, even to the opportunistic students who learn the ropes quickly. They have said to me, "Why study for a test? When you flunk, they let you take home the test and give you a chance to take the exact same one until you get at least a "C."

> **Character cannot develop where consequences are softened or removed.**

When negative consequences are waived due to our cultural conviction against pain and suffering the lesson that choices count is not learned. And since character is habit and habits are choices, character cannot develop where consequences are softened or removed.

Call for Restitution

For those people who have breathed in too deeply the ether of our culture which insists that "sorry's are good enough" the biblical story of Zaccheus serves as strong smelling salts to rouse us to moral clarity.

Zaccheus was a "wee little man" as the old Sunday School song says. What the song fails to mention is that he was a wee little man with a wee little conscience. He was a tax collector. You bemoan the fact that our income tax laws are complicated? Well, I'll take complicated, I'll take convoluted, I'll take confusing and frustrating any day over the system in Jesus' day.

As a tax collector Zaccheus had the power to extort; he could change your tax bracket at will. If Zaccheus felt like taking his wee little wife on a wee little trip for a long wee-kend he could upgrade his airline tickets to the first class cabin by a simple upgrade of your tax bill!

But when he encountered Jesus, something inside him said, "Enough!" He wanted to be a different man. Apparently he felt truly sorry about his life of greed, injustice and extortion. For when he elected to turn over a new leaf, he also committed himself to pay back everything he had squeezed out of John Q. Publican. What's more, he multiplied everything by four. This is a very significant decision. Under Jewish law, quadruple restitution was only necessary when an act of robbery included physical injury to the victim.

Presumably, Zaccheus had never harmed anyone while extorting money from his victims—wee little man that he was. However, he must have perceived his greed as egregious. Recognizing that he had been squeezing blood out of turnips, he felt his debt must be calculated by the full extent of the true harm he had caused.

In response to this unsolicited act of restitution, Jesus announced that salvation had come to Zaccheus.

And as much as Martin Luther might wish to brush off the sound of Jesus' pronouncement, lying as it does so uncomfortably close to the dreaded "salvation by works" heresy, we cannot escape how highly Jesus must have regarded this act of restitution.

Why is restitution so important?

First, it teaches the perpetrator that even when you say you're sorry, someone is still having to absorb the actual cost of the damage done. Even in the cases of honest accidents, like dinging someone's car door, "sorry" doesn't un-ding the door. In our culture, we want to think that it-was-just-an-accident beckons absolution. Moral character grows as people take full responsibility for the harm they cause, be it intentional or accidental.

Second, restitution is important because it reinforces the development of internal deterrents. Many years ago one of my nephews got angry and punched his fist into a wall. That was his first mistake. His second mistake was doing it when his grandpa was visiting. At his dad's prompting, Grandpa's upbringing sprang into action. Soon, my nephew and his grandpa were enjoying intergenerational bonding as they repaired the damage. My nephew did the labor under Grandpa's watchful and way-too-particular eye, and

> **Moral character grows as people take full responsibility for the harm they cause, be it intentional or accidental.**

55

paid for the materials out of his own pocket.

There haven't been any other holes in walls ever since.

Of course, there are times when it is also very appropriate to extend mercy and not make someone pay for the harm caused. But too many parents harm their children's moral development by the inhumane use of mercy.

Inhumane use of mercy? How can mercy ever be inhumane? Simple. Just as being nice by giving Johnny every toy he asks for will not be good for Johnny (i.e. he'll become a spoiled brat) even so extending mercy may be nice but not always good.

Finally, restitution is important because it offers mercy to the most deserving person. Please remember this: when you are extending mercy to the perpetrator, you are in effect choosing to withhold mercy from the victim. Only the victim has the right to make the offer to forego restitution. Otherwise, your responsibility is to side with the victim and insist on restitution.

Don't be misled into thinking that punishment and restitution pertain only to damaging offenses. On the contrary the most effective use of restitution can occur amid daily routines.

When Johnny (or you) knocks over a glass of milk, the one responsible should clean it up. If it's Suzy's week to take the trash to the curb, but she put it off and missed trash pickup day, she should have to take it out two weeks in a row (or something on that order.) Don't let these simple opportunities to teach restitution slip by unnoticed.

Speak a Reprimand

It's probably a good thing that children do not know what is often going on in an adult's mind when we give a reprimand. The reprimand would lose its sting to be sure, if they knew we were inwardly chuckling because we are remembering the times we were just like them. Or, if we are barely keeping the frown from arcing upward into a smile of pride about their clever mind. Or, if they knew we are only issuing a reprimand in order to register a mild warning to protect them—but we aren't really upset with them.

For many people reprimands are punishment enough. They hate the feeling of disapproval. Or, they hate what it feels like for certain people to disapprove.

I remember being reprimanded by my grandmother only once. But I remember it well, which shows what a reprimand can do. I was goofing around in the old camp meeting tabernacle at Adams Center, New York. I had lost interest in whatever was going on, which is to say the service was about five minutes old. The next thing I knew I felt a strong finger tap on my shoulder. I spun around to see my Grandma Schwab's rigid expression and hear her say, as if speaking into the microphone, "This is not how you behave in God's house."

Ordinarily, a straight line like that would have triggered a release of smart aleck punch lines in my mind. *Oh? I'm sorry. I didn't know He was home.* Or, *If this is His house, He should be able to buy some softer pews.* Instead, nothing else but blood rushed to my head. I felt my face burn with embarrassment and shame. A reprimand from Grandma meant I was barely one step away from being a juvenile delinquent.

But do you have to be a grandma before a reprimand has that level of impact? Not necessarily.

Of course, there are some kids (and adults) for whom reprimands seem to be as ineffective as a mousetrap in a lions den. But usually reprimands can have some effect provided they are healthy rather than unhealthy ones.

A healthy reprimand scolds the offender about the choice or act. It says," That was not a smart thing to do." Not, "How could you be so stupid?!" Unhealthy reprimands drag in something negative or critical about the person. Or worse, unhealthy reprimands open up the offender's entire rap sheet of past offenses. There is a reason why courts of law limit just how much of the defendant's prior record is admissible during the trial. It is generally agreed that it is unjust to do this.

Reprimands can have some effect provided they are healthy rather than unhealthy ones.

A healthy reprimand serves the welfare of the scoldee. It is not delivered to vent the frustration of the scolder. One of the unhealthiest, and consequently most ineffective, types of reprimand begins with the familiar, "I've had it up to here with you!" Walk through any discount superstore any day of the week any time of the day and you will hear this blurted out so many times you'd think it was a password to get an *additional 20% off* coupon. Unfortunately, these words are often delivered with a swat in such a way that you wonder which of the parties is the child.

A healthy reprimand is quick to restore normalcy. It assumes that once the words are spoken enough has been said. Things can go back to normal conversation and relating. Unhealthy reprimands tend to linger; silence and tension persists. The scolder smolders. Again, this deadens the effect of the reprimand. If the offender is conditioned to expect that more punishment is coming anyway, why pay attention to the reprimand? In his mind, it does no good.

When you violate any of these three principles of healthy reprimands frequently, you step into a vicious cycle that tends to make even healthy reprimands ineffective which then increases the likelihood that you will reprimand out of frustration. Everything gets unhealthier.

If this has happened in your home, you must go back to square one and start carefully rebuilding the woodshed consistently and methodically in each of these areas: apologies, consequences, restitution and reprimand. There is a powerful synergy when all four of these ingredients are mixed together. But take any one away and the effectiveness of the others is seriously reduced. For example, consider the diminishing impact over the course of time of allowing reprimands without consequences, consequences without apologies, or apologies without restitution.

———————

There is no doubt that the woodshed is perhaps the greatest missing ingredient in character development today. And there is also no doubt that it is doubly difficult to rebuild the woodshed surrounded by a culture that doesn't reinforce the enterprise of punishment.

There was a time when the general consensus in culture was that punishment was important, and that the community of parents were a team of players all agreeing to share the privilege of channeling one another's children toward good character. For example, that meant that every parent had tacit permission from every other parent to reprimand each other's children when they stepped out of line.

Used to be that any adult could speak to a child running through the church. Now just try it. You're liable to have an irate parent attacking you with a communion cup.

$\mathcal{R}$ECIPE $\mathcal{S}$TEPS: *WOODSHED*

▣ Don't be afraid of using punishment to shape character.

▣ Require sincere apologies, and make sure they are spoken sincerely and directly to the offended party.

▣ Impose consequences for wrong action and carry them out (most of the time) even when the consequence is received with a contrite spirit.

▣ Require that the offender make restitution in a way that is meaningful to both the offended person and the offender.

▣ Make effective use of healthy verbal reprimands, but be careful they don't become unhealthy.

Chapter Five

Ma'am

No one knows where the term smart aleck came from. Aleck is a nickname for Alexander. But who was the original Alexander, so brash and conceited that he would have inspired the origin of this epithet. No one knows. The original Alexander is not even a memory. But his spirit incarnated in me and in countless other teens and pre-teens since the term's humble beginning in the 1860's.

I had just enough wit to make myself laugh but not enough to know when to *ferme* my *la bouche*. Otherwise known as "shut my mouth." I thought I had a clever come back for everything. However, most of my clever come backs were concealed in my head and never trickled past my lips because of the restraining power of a surrounding culture that did not tolerate disrespect from children.

One day when I was in fourth grade I felt the power of that restraint from my gym teacher. I loved gym. Usually we played dodge ball or kickball. However, once a year we had to endure a brief exposure to something worse than the flu—square dancing. With girls.

This was the one time every year I was relieved to be part of my church denomination. Normally I viewed my church upbringing as more down than up. I bemoaned the fact that we couldn't go to movies or play sports on Sunday or enjoy life in general for fear we might be possessed by demons of liquor and loose women. But at least this one time each year it did me some good. All it took was an annual letter from my parents stating the denomination's conscientious objection to all forms of dancing, and I was excused. Whew!

Unfortunately—and I don't know what got into him—Mr. Mercer decided to have square dancing earlier than normal that year and did not give fair warning. So I did not have my letter procuring my dance deferment status. What was I to do? I tried to plead my case, but Mercer was merciless. It was too late. I was already in the gym and in my red gym shorts, the one's that smelled from weeks of unwashed incarceration in my wire basket number 197. The music was already blaring out of the battered record player with the bent needle, and he was already matching us up for ala man lefting and righting. But I couldn't go through with it. It was against my religion! Somehow I had to figure a way to doh-see-don't.

My solution was to turn it into a joke. That way I wasn't really dancing and could not be held accountable on the Judgment Day. When all the other boys were instructed, "Bow to your partner," I curtsied. When the caller chanted, "Promenade with your partner," I flounced and bounced like a drunken marionette. I laughed and hooted and hollered, which was not unlike the rest of the boys who had no convictions against the sins of social dancing. For some reason my protestant behavior was single-out-able, and before I could make it back around to my corner of the square, the full force of the teacher's hand struck the back of my head, permanently curing the cowlick problem that had plagued my hair for years.

I fell to the floor. Had the sky fallen? I turned around to the barking reprimand of my gym teacher telling me to shape up and quit goofing around. I said, "Yes sir." The spirit of smart aleck was effectively quenched. All it took was one swat. For the rest of the gym class I would have made Martin Luther proud the way I joined in the bacchanalian rounds and "sinned bravely."

Imagine that happening today. I can't even visualize the number of zeroes to the left of the decimal point of the dollar amount a family could be awarded today in a lawsuit if a gym teacher did what Mr. Mercer had done to me in 1963. More talk shows would whirl out of that one incident of "abuse" than tornadoes spawned by a hurricane hitting shore.

Certainly, I am not advocating that teachers use corporal punishment to control lack of respect. At least, maybe not swats on the back of the head. But there is nothing wrong with punishment for disrespect that is swift and measured—the size of an open palm at fifty miles an hour would be about the right speed and size if landing square across a young person's great divide. And I don't mean his mouth. The other great divide.

I know I may have just lost a few readers. I know that a great debate still rages over the use of corporal punishment with the pro-side being labeled barbarians by the con-side. I'm not dumb; I can read the nutrition facts on the side of a cereal box.

The purpose of this chapter is not to engage in a defense of corporal punishment or deny the claim that "Physical punishment creates abusive people." However, it cannot be denied that, whatever we are doing, we are not training kids to be respectful. The problems associated with disrespect are enormous today. Isn't it interesting that the term smart aleck did not even originate, probably due to the behavior of just one social deviant, until the mid nineteenth century? Today "smart aleckiness" is the social norm.

The horrifying results of a culture that has spared the rod are evident all around. Kids snarl at any adult who dares to correct them. Treating another person with enough respect to be careful and tactful is now branded as dishonest in our "reality show" television culture.

> **Disrespectful behavior must be exterminated with the same zeal and sense of urgency we direct toward termites. If not, the framework of social structures will be eaten away.**

Respectful behavior is no longer being expected and demanded. Any effort to re-create a character development culture must take seriously the challenge of restoring the missing ingredient of respect. Disrespectful behavior must be exterminated with the same zeal and sense of urgency we direct toward termites. If not, the framework of social structures will be eaten away.

Use Personal Titles.

It is almost universally understood that respect is shown through addressing elders and people of position by their proper titles. You never say this to a judge, "Hey, what about my client?" You say, "Your honor, if it pleases the court, I would like to talk to you about my client."

However, there are fewer and fewer situations when this approach is required. Children used to be required to address their elders as Mister Jones or Missus Jones. Even friends of the family were protected from disrespect by insisting that the children refer to adults as Uncle Bill and Aunt Jean, even if they weren't blood relatives. After a father finished words of advice or reprimand with the question, "Do you understand?" the only proper response was, "Yes sir." Today a dad is lucky to get a grunt of acknowledgment, even if he manages to get Billy to take off the headphones while he's talking.

I readily admit that I have contributed to the near extinction of these forms of respect. As a young pastor, I was very uncomfortable with my role as a "spiritual leader." I did not seek nor feel qualified for the job. I also brought with me a profound distaste for the over-lording I saw too often accompanying the clerical position. I wanted my people to see me as one of "them." I didn't want to be distant. So I invited people to "Call me Doug." Not Reverend Newton. Not Pastor Newton. Not the syrupy Pastor Doug. That sounds like I should be wearing a ten gallon cowboy hat and a big silver badge. None of that for me. Just call me Doug. Wow, was I accessible! I was so accessible even the four year old boys that dive bomb the sanctuary after morning services would call me Doug right after barking words, "Out of the way!" while barreling between my legs chasing whatever little boys chase.

I see no way around it. Addressing people properly is a form of respect that works like a comb stroking unkempt hair. Steady use over time trains the words to lay correctly and more presentably. And with the training of the words, the attitude follows.

Some people may argue that this approach forces kids into a subservient role which can stifle their self expression. Exactly.

Make Eye Contact.

I think a government subsidized study should be conducted to isolate the behavioral disorder that afflicts most young people. If we believe that there is such a thing as ADD (Attention Deficit Disorder) for children who can't focus on the chalk board, and BDD (Behavioral Deficit Disorder) for children who punch other children on the playground, then certainly there is a treatable disorder that explains why kids no longer look you in the eye when they talk to you. The government should step in. Add an ECDD program to the list. Eye Contact Deficit Disorder. While they are at it they should add a program for EDD (Enunciation Deficit Disorder) to help kids who mumble.

Excuse me for speaking out, but things are getting ridiculous. Pretty soon there will be more "deficit disorders" than there are elements in the universe.

We could probably argue all day about the validity of diagnoses like ADD and their treatment, but there is no reason why young people can't be taught and expected to look someone in the eyes. "Look, at me when we are talking" should be the first thing that a parent says before any conversation, like reading the Miranda Rights.

This is not a radical concept. It is simply a technique for requiring respectful behavior that was employed effectively for generations. Admittedly, during the course of any five minute conversation with an untrained teen, the imperative "Look at me" has to be repeated numerous times. Keeping a child's head from sinking into his lap is often as difficult as holding a boiled pasta noodle upright. However, the effort is worth it. Children who learn to look people in the eye are a joy to talk with no matter what they are saying, because you get the privilege of talking to a human being. Meeting a person eye to eye is that important! It is not an accident that certain tribal groups look for the sign of a person's soul in the eyes. There is a connection that occurs during eye contact; it is the on ramp to mutual respect.

> **There is a connection that occurs during eye contact; it is the on-ramp to mutual respect.**

Don't Interrupt.

One final forgotten technique for teaching respect is to prohibit interruptive behavior. If there ever is an example of a lost element of respect it is this area. Children have little hope of learning not to interrupt if they watch adults behave. Politicians scream at each other. Talk shows improve their ratings to the degree their "issues" prompt jeers from a frenzied audience that drowns out discussion. The preferred protest method of those who claim their right to free speech is to drown out the speech of others. Ironic.

This has not been the case until recently. Thirty years ago if a child walked between two adults standing in conversation, he would have been grabbed by the shoulder and given a mid-course correction around the conversants rather than between. The adult conversation would have stopped momentarily as this lesson was administered. Sibling arguments were officiated by adult referees who did not hesitate to call encroachment and illegal procedure fouls when one child did not wait for the other to finish. And if the offender could not restrain himself, he was pulled from the field of discussion and sat down on the bench of silence.

This is not a radical technique or a fascinating secret. Most readers are probably nodding with faint recognition of these forgotten ways, like an amnesiac experiences flashes of almost remembering who he is. And probably those who are remembering are agreeing with the importance of learning not to interrupt. We have each experienced all too often being cutoff in mid sentence. We have felt the corrosive effect on our sense of worth when another person isn't interested enough in our thoughts to follow them through to their conclusion. We agree with the importance, but we just don't remember to insist on non-interruptive behavior in our kids.

The missing ingredient of requiring respectful behavior must be inserted back into the cultural mix.

It is the ingredient that requires the most meticulous and consistent attention of all. Respectful forms of address. Eye contact. No interrupting. The chances of going wrong in these areas are so numerous, because the occasions requiring them are so frequent. But insist we must.

Is there something wrong with "compliance?"

Some people may argue, "What good is insisting on these behaviors? All they produce is compliance." To be sure these are just external measures that do not guarantee anything more than compliance and the appearance of respect, but is there anything wrong with mere compliance? People talk as if compliance is to moral behavior as Ishmael (Abraham's ill begotten son) is to Isaac (the son conceived the "right way."). Compliance, they say, is the wrong way to create acceptable behavior. Let me rescue compliance from the ranks of the illegitimate.

Ultimately, any worthwhile moral development depends on individual choice. An individual must decide whether he will "buy into" the values of his particular group. No group can guarantee that all its individuals will do so. If a majority fails to embrace shared values, the group will cease to be a cohesive group and fall apart.

The purpose of compliance is to create a grand demonstration of those values, to illustrate how the group values are supposed to look. The goal of compliance is like the goal of shopping for a dress for the prom. How do you know if you want it unless you try it on? "Forcing" kids to behave according to certain standards, even if they aren't "doing it from the heart" is both necessary and commendable. It is necessary because kids will not tend to act respectfully. It is commendable because through strategies of compliance a cultural group is doing its best to show what it values. This is who we are. This is how we think you should behave.

> **Through strategies of compliance a cultural group is doing its best to show what it values.**

Compliance, which is often rejected because it makes kids do something contrary to their true heart, turns out to be the most honest thing we can do for our young people. Mere compliance is not a satisfactory goal of character development. But working toward compliance is the most effective means of disclosing what we value.

Teaching young people the habit of showing respect is especially important in a world that offers everyone the technological capability of placing himself in the center of the universe with the ability to have everything custom made to personal preferences. Let's take a close look at this new technological world and the formidable challenge it presents to character development.

$\mathcal{R}$*ECIPE* $\mathcal{S}$*TEPS:* **MA'AM**

▣ Teaching respect requires vigilance. Never let down.

▣ All disrespectful comments, tones of voice, facial expressions, and body language should be confronted and eliminated.

▣ Teach children to address people appropriately.

▣ Require eye contact when you are in conversation.

▣ Do not allow children to interrupt or disrupt conversation.

▣ Form alliances with other parents and adults, granting one another permission to require respectful behavior from each other's children.

▣ Don't be afraid of shooting for compliance. It is not necessary at first that a child understand and appreciate respectful standards of behavior, just that they follow those standards as a definition of our common value on respectfulness.

▣ Engage in an experimental period of a month when you require a child to respond, "Yes, sir" or "Yes, ma'am."

Chapter Six

Black and White TV

I don't remember life without television. But I do remember life without color television. For years Ed Sullivan's show entertained me and my family with his "really big shooow" and introduced us to the latest and greatest, the prettiest and wittiest without the benefit of hue and saturation.

On Saturday night my older brother and I waited for the once a month Errol Flynn movie. We would feast on TV dinners—an incredible new miracle of technology—and swashbuckle our way through mashed potatoes along with Captain Blood. But the blood was never red. Fighting men lived and fought and died heroically in pools of gray.

By today's standards of entertainment we were impoverished. But it never felt like it to us, because we didn't know any better... that is until *Bonanza*.

Bonanza spoiled everything in such a pleasant way. A television show created specifically to sell color televisions, *Bonanza* accomplished its mission in our family —eventually. But not for an agonizing couple of years after we first watched *Bonanza* in color at the Juhlin's one Sunday night following church. Larry Juhlin worked for GE and was able to get one of the first models.

We watched—one time is all it took—and nothing was ever the same. From that moment on we begged to have a color TV in our home, "Dad, please, Dad, please, Dad, please, Dad, please!"

Almost overnight our entire nation became discontent with anything less than the next and the best instrument for giving us "real" experiences in entertainment.

My! What we could do with technology!

Our new swashbuckling spirit of technology helped us push through the once impenetrable shroud of gravity to float on the empty sea of space toward the moon. We built crafts that could crawl the deepest ocean floor. We atomically sharpened our natural 20:20 vision and peered for the first time into microscopic worlds of matter. The final frontier was the world of limitations—and we were conquering it.

Technology was not really about science. It was about religion. It was about setting human beings free from all restrictions. Reaching for divinity. It was about having anything, making anything possible, and deifying the human will with the power to choose from among unlimited options.

Before long the typi-cal neighborhood grocery stores became stocked with 20 brands of catsup. And then one morning we all woke up to a consumer

> • • • • • • • • • • • • • •
> **We became a nation of**
> **people accustomed to**
> **having exactly what we**
> **want when we**
> **want it.**
> • • • • • • • • • • • • • •

world overtaken by steroid-injected Wal-Marts become muscle-bound Super Wal-Marts.

All that from *Bonanza* in color?

Yes—metaphorically, at least, if not literally. We be-came a nation of people accustomed to having exactly what we want when we want it.

The world of choice was once binary. Decisions usually involved choosing between two options. Either Keds or PF Flyers. Either Coke or Pepsi. Either McDon-alds hamburgers or cheeseburgers. Which of the two will it be?

Now ironically the binary world of computeriza-tion has made possible a consumer world of exponen-tial options. The consumer mind is psychometrically plotted and graphed. The marketplace is meticulously studied and segmented; products and packaging are intricately customized to give every person the perfect match between consumer goods and personal prefer-ence.

Through the miracle of worldwide databasing

manufacturers no longer need to believe in or search desperately for the holy grail of the "average consumer." Products can now be tailor-made on demand. Car buyers can design their future car on-line.

But what happens to moral character when people are conditioned to expect that they can have any product customized to fit exactly the nuances of their personal taste?

Character and Malleability

Never before in history has it been possible for the self to be the anvil around which options are hammered. The outer world of choices can be reshaped to fit "me."

Until fifty years ago things were the other way around. The self had to reshape and bend and adjust to fit the limited options available. A person had to be flexible – or what is often referred to as "malleable."

You don't like peas? Too bad. That's what's on your plate. Learn to like them. These lyrics were a national anthem sung in every home nightly.

Now the anthem we raise is *Who wants what?* at the food court, or as we open the freezer and pullout microwavable entrées.

This is a serious problem, because it undermines the development of malleability. To be malleable is to be like clay—able to be shaped by the influence of external forces and circumstances. And when that trait is missing, there is little hope for any moral growth.

In this sense malleability is not only a character trait but what we might call a mechanical cause of character development. It is a trait that makes movement toward other traits possible.

> A person conditioned to expect everything to fit his personal preferences will become a moral couch potato.

Getting up off the couch is a mechanical cause of physical fitness. No person will ever develop physical traits of strength, endurance and flexibility if he never turns off the T.V. and goes outside to work or exercise.

Similarly, a person conditioned to expect everything to fit his personal preferences will become a moral couch potato lacking the will and ability to flex and adjust to the very circumstances that could produce improved character traits. So it stands to reason that malleability must be developed. How can that happen?

The "Options Diet"

Can we agree with the simple argument that having one hundred different flavors of soft drink tends to support the outcome that people don't have to learn to be flexible and adjust? Can we agree that when kids are used to having 50 options at McDonalds they tend to become more whiny about having just what they want? And if they are told their only choice is between a hamburger and a fish sandwich you can expect them to put up a fuss.

If we can agree on that then the course of action is self-evident. A big step toward creating malleability is taken by simply limiting the number of options a person has.

At this point I must pause to highlight a distinction that might be slipping past you unnoticed. But it is a vital distinction as I propose the strategy of limiting options.

In our modern usage of the English language, most people use the words "choices" and "options" interchangeably. But it is not correct to do so. A choice is what you make. The options are what you have to choose among.

Suppose your family sits down for a meal at a local restaurant and looks at a menu with 20 items. It is common to hear someone say, "Look at all these choices." Or, "Wow! Look at all the choices you kids have." This is not the correct use of the word "choice." You see, in that situation you are not wanting the kids to make several choices. You only want them to make one choice from among the many options available.

It is good practice to give kids choices. But malleability is increased when you limit the number of options the kids have to choose from.

Here's how it can work. The next time you go to the food court at the mall, don't let everyone go running off to their favorite fast food establishment. You know the routine. You're giving one kid ten dollars to go to McDonalds. You're giving the next kid ten dollars to go to the pizza place. Then you tell everybody to meet back at the food court clock to eat, hoping that everyone will get back at approximately the same time so you can have some semblance of a "family meal" together.

Instead, pick one fast food place from which everyone will get food. Stick to your guns no matter how much opposition you face. Yea though you walk through the valley of the shadow of death, fear no evil and stick to your guns! Then have each kid choose from among the "more than enough" options at that one establishment. Each one still gets to make his own choice, but the number of options is severely limited. Each one has to learn to find something he or she likes at the one option that has been given.

Do you think that will be hard to do? The degree of difficulty is in inverse proportion to the degree of malleability of the kids. The harder the prospect of carrying out this plan seems to you the less malleable your kids probably are. And consequently the more crucial it is that you take measures like this.

I don't want to meddle, but you might want to try this technique on yourself as well. We all can use some practice in malleability from time to time, because we get so used to having hundreds of options as well.

For example, why not try unplugging the cable TV

with its 150 channels and live for one month on only the six or seven channels that float into your house through the airwaves.

Once you catch onto this idea of limiting options you'll see hundreds of opportunities for cutting back on your options every week. You don't have to do that all the time. But you need to put your household on an "options diet" regularly if you hope to combat the cultural overabundance of options that prevents the development of malleability.

If you think the "options diet" seems hard, wait until you hear my next suggestion.

Limit Choices

If having a limited number of options improves the chances of developing malleability, that method can't hold a candle to the technique of limiting the number of choices. (Don't forget the distinction between choices and options.) Yes, I really mean "choices" this time.

Fifty years ago when Mom served supper, it was an event characterized by a nearly absolute lack of choices, not just a lack of options. There was Swiss steak—and no choice about it—for supper. There were French cut green beans... and no choice about it. There was only one question: "Do you want water?" And even that wasn't really a choice, because it was always being asked as Mom was already pouring the water!

Somehow along the way of the American journey

toward freedom and individualism we have adopted the idea that personal choice equals personal freedom, and therefore to take away the privilege to choose is to take away freedom. It is true that having a choice is one of the treasured elements of freedom. But choice is not equivalent with freedom, nor is having a choice a guarantee that you will have freedom.

> **There is nothing necessarily wrong or unloving or dictatorial about denying a person the opportunity to choose.**

Nevertheless, that is what most people believe, especially the young. If you take away my right to choose, you take away my freedom.

In addition, the freedom to choose is also associated with self-expression. If you take away my ability to choose, you somehow diminish me; you violate my selfhood; you injure my spirit.

Our culture has bought into that idea so much that we regard the removal of choice as a form of abuse.

We have to get over this naïve notion about the intrinsic value of choice and its power to automatically provide the individual with freedom or a healthy sense of self. Like fire, choice has the power for good or ill. It is not intrinsically beneficial. There is nothing necessarily wrong or unloving or dictatorial about denying a person the opportunity to choose. On the contrary, taking away a persons right to choose can often be the most loving thing to do depending on the situation.

For example, when a child is three years old a wise and loving parent will not let him choose when to cross a busy street. In that situation it is far more loving that a parent should take away his choice than a car should take away his life. When the child is five a wise parent will begin to give the child freedom to try making that choice on his own. But even then the parent will retain the right to veto an unwise choice.

If this is obviously the loving thing to do when it comes to young children crossing the street, why shouldn't it also be the case anytime a person—no matter what age they are—does not have enough knowledge, experience or common sense to make a wise decision on their own.

In other words it is not necessarily demeaning or dictatorial to deny a person the opportunity to choose. There are all sorts of good reasons to limit a person's privilege of choice—say, for example, when trying to develop a person's character.

And this brings us back to our strategy of increasing malleability by limiting the privilege of choice.

One of the greatest attributes of character is the ability to recognize and humbly receive those situations and circumstances that are beyond a person's control. The famous Serenity Prayer used since the 1940s by Alcoholics Anonymous says it so well, "God, grant me the serenity to accept the things I cannot change..."

To be sure, for most people who lack character there are way too many times when they give up too quickly and just assume, "There's nothing I can do." But this is another matter—a matter of resourcefulness and courage that I will address in the chapter on hand-me-downs.

The fact still remains that many things in life must be accepted and endured bravely in the knowledge that you have no choice in the matter.

Therefore, it is wise to teach people how to handle the absence of the privilege of choice. But when and how do you do that?

In the home and family context you have some wonderful opportunities to create malleability and teach values at the same time by the very nature of what you stipulate as nonnegotiable. For example, when you establish a priority of sitting down to supper or breakfast together, you create the situation during which you will say over and over again, "You can't do such and such, because eating together is what our family does. Sorry, but you don't have a choice in the matter."

> **Many things in life must be accepted and endured bravely in the knowledge that you have no choice in the matter.**

The more your family's values become fixed, the more opportunities you will have to limit choices, not capriciously or arbitrarily, but meaningfully.

Similarly, if you are married, your children can learn a lot about dealing with limited choices by the way you position your marriage in relation to your kids. Unfortunately, many marriages are child-centric. Mom and Dad adjust and bend to fit the desires and schedules of the kids. Look who's becoming malleable.

Kids do not need to be the center of the family system. That's like the sun revolving around the moon. Rather, every family should revolve around the sunlight of a strong husband-wife relationship. Every home should be marriage-centric.

When our daughters were quite small, we set them inside a red wagon and went for a daily walk. But the walk was only secondarily for them. Primarily, it was time for my wife and me to walk and talk. We connected. We reviewed the day. We planned the week. We held hands. And our girls watched from behind.

They had no choice. We did not ask them each afternoon if they preferred going for a walk at that time. No, my wife and I believed one of our greatest gifts to them was a Mom and Dad who loved each other. This was a gift we could only give if, in fact, we cultivated our love relationship through these daily routines of connection and conversation. They had no choice but to go with that flow.

Our strong convictions and family values created those kind of opportunities when it made sense even to young children why they had no choice. And then as they grew older, they embraced those values and also understood the benefits and reasons why having no other choice can often be a good thing.

If you are a single parent, you can still create essentially the same teachable moments by setting aside time for yourself to walk and talk with God, or improve your mind through reading. You can insist on the kids observing your "quiet time" during which they must wait for your attention.

Another perfect opportunity to teach malleability through limiting choice occurs when "plans change." Every adult knows that you have to be ready to "go with the flow." You can do your best to plan your schedule down to the minute. But if one piece of the sequence is delayed or falls through, everything has to shift. Plans have to change. You have no choice. You may have to delete something you hoped to do.

In the same way, plans often have to do with money. You may have a great vacation planned, but if the car's transmission goes out, you may have to spend $1200 to fix the car instead and forego the vacation. These changes are disappointing, and yet can be the very occasions during which flexibility is created.

At those times, when you really have no choice, you can learn or teach flexibility in the very act of going back to the drawing board and creating Plan B. In fact, malleability requires a stalwart determination not to be thwarted. Malleability is not mere acceptance as in surrender. Malleability is more like a team going into the locker room at halftime ten points down, very aware that they have no choice about the way things are, but resolve to figure out a new strategy for the second half.

So in the context of home life, it is wise to challenge children with a question at the point of having no choice. They will often moan when they hear it, because of how often they will hear it. But that is all the more reason to ask it: *what can you do to make the most of this situation?*

"I know you are disappointed that you got sick and can't go to the party, but what can you do to make the most of it?" Too often parents step in too soon to try to ease the pain of the disappointing situation by offering a substitute. This is not necessarily bad, but they're losing a great opportunity to engage the child in practicing a flexible attitude and creative thinking.

Perhaps you are beginning to see the compounding interrelationships between the last several chapters. Anyone in a role of shaping character has to be willing to employ or allow pain in the process. There is an unpleasant irony in this. The very fact that you are engaged in character development means that you deeply love your child, which makes the prospect of inflicting pain all the more heart wrenching.

However, Jack Fuller, President of the Tribune Company which owns the historic *Chicago Tribune* newspaper, offers this advice to leaders, which also serves as sound wisdom for parents, too:

> *"Anybody who is going to be a leader* [think, parent] *has to be prepared to inflict pain on occasion. You hope you're doing it wisely and thoughtfully and without anger. But if you're not prepared to do it at all, you probably ought to leave your role."*
>
> Best Practices: The Art of Leadership in
> News Organizations

Are you willing to keep going? There's still more missing ingredients we need to face. Closely related to this world of unlimited options that diminishes malleability is a world that shies away from deprivation and fails to create gratitude.

ℛECIPE ⑨TEPS:
BLACK AND WHITE TV

▣ Develop malleable people—people who can adjust to disappointing situations and think creatively about a new approach.

▣ Understand the difference between options and choices, but still intentionally limit both.

▣ Practice making choices from among three options rather than ten.

▣ Don't cave in when kids feel deprived of their favorite options.

▣ Give people an opportunity to adjust to having no choice about the way something is or what they will have available.

▣ Establish immovable family convictions which create occasions when we give ourselves and our families no choice.

▣ Use occasions when people have no choice as an opportunity to be flexible enough to find other options.

Chapter Seven

Cold Peas

I think I was 23 years old the first time I ever ate warm vegetables. Surprisingly, they weren't half bad. This was a considerable improvement over any previous experience with vegetables, which had always been all bad.

I can't explain my innate aversion to vegetables. True, their environment of origin is dirt, seasoned with animal waste and the by-products of decomposition aided by various species of wriggling insects. But none of these elements is held in contempt by young boys. On the contrary, they are held in curiosity, and then stored in jars and pants pockets. If anything, the location of vegetables' upbringing should have given them an endearing quality.

But that made no difference. I hated vegetables. Which, in point of fact, made no difference to my mom who always made me take some as they were passed around the table each night. And if I happened to short-change myself, my mom would personally, I dare say gleefully, ladle more onto my plate until I had taken the minimum daily requirement recommended by my own personal Food and Drug Administrator.

Well, as we all know, you can lead a horse to water, but you can't make him eat the peas. So every night the peas sat there until rigor mortis set in.

And so did I.

My aversion to vegetables began early and lasted through several growth spurts and a complete change of prepositions. It started when I was small enough to be told I could not get *down* from the table until I had eaten my vegetables. And it lasted until I was told I could not get *up* from the table until I had finished my vegetables.

Ultimately each night, I ate my cold peas because I knew my life was on hold until I did. Nothing could budge my mom's resolve to deprive me of any of life's hopes and dreams if the peas were still on my plate. Dessert. TV. I couldn't even bribe her with a trade-off. An extra half–hour of piano practice for a cold peas re-prieve. I have no doubt but what she would have de-layed even my wedding day until I had finished my peas.

Happily, my mom and dad never used the "starv-ing kids in China" argument on me. History books re-

cord this being used since time immemorial, way before there was even a China in which to find starving
children. And still it has never, ever worked. Instead,
they simply threatened me with becoming one of those
starving kids.

Deprivation is what this technique is called.

With Archimedean effect, deprivation is the ful-
crum point used to lift people toward the character
trait of gratitude. And like Archimedes, parents would
be shouting, "Eureka!" around the world if they ever
discovered this powerful leverage.

Parents throughout the ages have always known
how having to go without some thing helps a person
value that thing. Absence makes the heart grow fonder
whether pertaining to family or food. Deprivation is a
platonic aphrodisiac.

However, our culture is not deprivation friendly. A
wealthy society that puts the satisfying of desires within the reach of a remote control or
credit card accustoms us to having what we want when we want
it. To be deprived of anything due
to unfortunate circumstances feels
like the world has turned against
us. To be deprived due to the intentional actions of others is considered cruel and inhumane treatment.

> **Deprivation is both under-experienced and under-used in character development.**

So deprivation is both under-experienced and
underused in character development. If our children,

93

or even our adult population, are ever to become grateful people they must know the absence of privileges and the experience of unfulfilled desires on a regular basis.

Gratitude: The Trait with Amnesia

In the Old Testament, God's people were warned time and again about forgetting the "wonderful deeds of the Lord." Sure enough, within a short span of time they forgot about their marvelous miraculous deliverance from Egypt and the daily supernatural provision of manna to eat. They grumbled about their diet, as if manna were nothing more than cold peas. How quickly they forgot to be grateful.

To counteract this tendency to slip into ingratitude, God recommended seasons and ceremonies of deprivation as reminders that their current life style was a privilege not a right. For example, the annual Feast of Booths put them back in touch with what it was like to wander in the wilderness with no permanent homes.

In the same way, parents who want to stimulate gratitude must use deprivation routinely, not as punishment, but simply on general principles. For example, if it has become routine to watch TV on a big screen, spend a week watching TV on the old 21-inch in the closet.

My good friend's family, with three growing boys, annually eats only rice dishes during the entire month of February.

94

Occasionally suspend cell phone privileges, or take away the headphones for a couple days, or don't go to the mall for a month for no other reason than "just because." It's not punishment. It's development. Your kids won't like it. A sure sign you are on the right track.

Gratitude Expressed is Golden

One of the saddest forms of poverty among people is the lack of expressing and hearing gratitude.

I once worked alongside a fine colleague who had sacrificed a great deal in his life to serve an international church organization. You would think, of all places, a religious organization should be especially adept at expressing gratitude. Yet this high-level executive told me that his superiors had never spoken thanks to him one time in his ten year term. That is, of course, not including his retirement reception during which woefully inadequate attempts were made to compensate for what was left too long unsaid.

If there is any place the golden rule should rule our behavior it is in this area of gratitude.

Everyone knows the golden rule. *Do unto others as you would have them do unto you.* Notice how the golden rule turns on the pivot verb *would have.* Question: When do you *would have*?

Do you *would have* when a person is doing what you *would have* them do to you? Of course not, because they are already doing it. The only time your mind gives any attention to "would having" is when someone is not doing what you *would have* them do to you. It is at that time when our minds grow troubled by— even obsessed with—what someone is not doing for us. But according to the golden rule, at the very time they are not giving you what you *would have* you are supposed to give that very thing to them. Wow! That's what makes the rule golden!

So the golden rule of gratitude reads: *Express gratitude unto others as you would have them express gratitude unto you.* But because we typically want to be thanked and wait to be thanked more than we think of thanking, we all contribute to a relatively thankless world.

Gratitude is hard to develop in a thank-deprived world. That's why we all need to make a profound commitment to expressing gratitude ourselves and insisting that gratitude is expressed to others.

For example, deprivation should be employed when young people fail to express thanks. This is a telltale sign of the lack of gratitude. The old remedy for the failure to say "thank you" was to suspend the privilege temporarily. Just like eating cold peas, children should be required to say thank you's in every instance one is merited. Of course this means it should become the language of your heart as well.

> **We typically want to be thanked and wait to be thanked more than we think of thanking.**

The fact is, just like self-fulfilling prophecies, there is a reflexive property about gratitude. When gratitude expresses itself, it actually increases itself.

Gratitude and Copper Pennies

Way back when I was in junior high a kid would get mocked if he dared pick up a stray penny on the floor. In fact, it was not uncommon for gangs of boys to toss pennies down the school corridor just to laugh at anyone who bent over to get one. "You must be so poor that you have to pick up pennies! Ha! Ha! Ha!"

Of course, we would never treat our children that way. However, we still have a tendency to teach them not to value what the world considers valueless.

For example, look at how we observe Christmas today compared to seventy-five years ago. How many of our children would be thrilled to get an orange and a few pieces of licorice in their stocking these days? Yet for many kids of days gone by, that was a tremendous treat. That was Christmas.

Today kids' Christmas lists are more like catalogues. Parents develop a peculiar fear around Christmastime each year. Out-of-stock a phobia drives them to rush to toy stores like they're landing on Omaha beach.

This annual Christmas fear of not giving their kids what the other kids are getting actually survives the holidays and emerges throughout the year as parents cart their kids to sports and all the activities the other kids are involved in. Families are no longer trying to keep up with the Joneses, they're trying to keep their kids up with the Joneses kids!

One way to restore a sense of gratitude in such a rich culture is to keep yourself and your family living well below the level of standard expectations. If the other kids participate in three sports, have your kids pick only one. If you have been in the habit of spending $500 per child at Christmas, cut that in half. If they are used to getting three or four "big" gifts on their birthday, give only one.

As long as their attention is focused on having what all the other kids have, children will never be grateful for the particulars they do have.

Of course, it probably isn't good to suddenly cut back without some kind of explanation and substitute value in the place of what's being deprived. For example, you can expose children to the experience of actual deprivation. You do this by keeping them conscious of kids and families that have very little. It is not hard for children to feel empathy, and from that point, believe it or not, it is a small step to engage them in voluntary self-deprivation to help those families.

So for example, this Christmas you might consider cutting your gift budget in half and using the money you saved to serve those who are in need. Involve the kids in the process of exploring options and making plans.

Or, when you save time by limiting your kids extra-curricular activities to one sport, you can expose them to people who can't even walk much less play a sport. Then use some of the time you save by doing yardwork for an elderly widow.

All in all, the development of gratitude requires consistent emphasis on the blessings of even the smallest and most common things, one pea at a time. And if necessary, deprivation may be the only path.

As it turns out deprivation is a versatile tool in character development, not only because it inspires gratitude. It also lies behind one of the most under-appreciated character traits, and consequently one of the rarest, as we shall see in the next chapter.

$\mathcal{R}$*ECIPE* $\mathcal{S}$*TEPS:* **COLD PEAS**

- ▣ Use the technique of deprivation to engender gratitude.

- ▣ No matter what our culture says the absence of privileges and the experience of unfulfilled desires is not cruel and inhumane punishment.

- ▣ It is easy to forget to be grateful, so seasons of intentional deprivation (e.g. a week without television or music or sweets) should be observed routinely.

- ▣ Insist on people saying specific and frequent thank you's. Gratitude is not true gratitude until it is expressed.

- ▣ Teach people to place more value in the things the world considers of little worth.

- ▣ Emphasize the blessings of even the smallest and most common things.

Chapter Eight

Hand-Me-Downs

I am a middle child. I have an older brother and a younger brother. Don't worry, I am not one of those people who think that everything from personality to life purpose is determined by *birth order.*

But as a middle child, the most significant birth order influence on my life was that I was always in line for the clothes my brother had worn before me. They were called hand me downs, which is a misnomer because I never once requested that anyone "hand me" those clothes. I got his shirts, his pants, his sneakers. Fortunately he wore out his underwear quicker than I could grow into them or I'm sure I would walk today with a severe nervous twitch from years of secretly tugging at sagging briefs with limp elastic waist bands.

Our family engaged in the ritual not because we were poor and could not afford new clothing every growing spurt. In fact, my dad, manager of a factory, pulled in enough money annually to afford placing the type of sound system speakers (Klipsch LaScala) in our living room that were also used in Radio City Music Hall. Every two years he picked out a new car from one of the automobile factories orbiting Detroit. The car and all gas (even for personal use) was purchased by the company.

Our family engaged in the ritual because hand me downs were P.C. — Parentally Correct. It was part of a cultural mindset that did not have to be taught or justified.

- *Don't throw away "perfectly good" things.*
- *Get as much use out of something as you can.*
- *Darn those socks.*

(You younger readers may think I just mildly cursed a pair of socks. "Darning" socks means fixing a hole in the toe or heel.)

Hand me downs represented a form of self-imposed deprivation that refused to discard what could still be used. It was planned non-obsolescence. Just as a "governor" on an accelerator keeps a driver from driving a vehicle too fast, hand-me-downs place a governor on throwing things out too fast.

As a result, this hand-me-down conviction against the throw-away impulse tended to create the often overlooked but extremely valuable character trait of resourcefulness.

Resourcefulness pertains to making the most of our opportunities and our possessions.

Choose Wisely

Hand me downs represent a time when the word "everything" contained fewer things. There were fewer options, fewer opportunities, fewer brands of cereal, fewer restaurants and motels, fewer television channels, fewer books and magazines, fewer government programs, fewer things to do after school, fewer styles, fewer... everything.

A few years ago I received a letter from some good friends who were traveling around the world speaking to student mission groups. One letter describing their experience and upcoming itinerary included this striking sentence:

> "From Kinchase we go to Nairobi where we must catch a plane to Mombassa. If we miss it there won't be another for six days."

Imagine the dumbfounded reaction of an American accustomed to the multitude of flights departing every minute from the big cities in America being told another plane would not be along for six days.

We have so many options, so many opportunities that we have become conditioned to treat our choices lightly. After all, if we forget or procrastinate or choose poorly another opportunity will be along shortly. It's no big deal. If we have other things on our mind so that we forget to pick up milk on the way home, no problem. We can run out to the Minit Mart after supper.

The proliferation of options has diminished the sense of urgency about choosing wisely. We have too many third and fourth chances to get things right. We are not compelled to be careful and make the most of every opportunity.

In order to develop the trait of resourcefulness, we must choreograph our children's world with opportunities that reintroduce the sense: "You have only one chance to take advantage of this opportunity. Choose wisely."

How does this work?

First, *break the habit of giving multiple reminders.* Parents love their kids and do not want them to miss out on good opportunities, so they fall into the counterproductive habit of taking on their child's responsibility to remember.

(On Tuesday morning.)

"Johnny, don't forget to fill out you registration form for the field trip. The deadline is tomorrow."

"O.K. Mom."

(On Tuesday afternoon.)

"Johnny. Did you turn in your registration?"

"No. I forgot."

"Well, make sure you get that done tonight."

(On Tuesday at bedtime.)

"Johnny, did you do your registration?"

"In a minute, Mom."

(On Wednesday morning.) "Johnny, got your registration form?"

"Oh no! I started but didn't finish it!

"Well, hurry upstairs and get it."

"O.K... Oh no. I can't. The bus is coming!"

"Where did you leave it?" Mom calls out as Johnny rushes to the bus. "I'll finish it for you and drop it off later at school..."

Giving multiple reminders is a big mistake if you want to develop resourceful people who value opportunities and make the most of them.

A local college admissions counselor recently told me of a mother who offered to pay him a hundred dollars a month to wake her son up every morning so he would go to class. Apparently her years of multiple reminders had become nothing more than a snooze alarm for this young man.

Second, in order to teach young people the importance of making the most of opportunities, you must *enforce forfeiture*. In the scenario above, mom finally finished Johnny's registration form and actually took it to school for him so he wouldn't miss out on the field trip.

What do you think this taught Johnny? That his choice to put off his responsibility had no consequence. It would have been better—though harder—for Mom to simply let Johnny miss out.

Forfeiture is the school marm of resourcefulness.

In days gone by it was commonplace for people to have these kinds of frequent thoughts:

- *If I don't figure out a way to patch the soles of my shoes, I won't have any shoes to wear.*
- *If I don't figure out a way to come up with an extra five dollars, I won't be able to get my medicine this month.*
- *If I don't figure out some way to get the tractor running, the crop is going to spoil.*

In days gone by the prospect of real forfeiture drove people to take advantage of the least little opportunity, possibility, or resource. Necessity truly was the mother of invention, and she had lots of children.

Today, the risk of forfeiture is not so commonplace and automatic. So that risk must be inserted manually. You can't be afraid to let children miss their one chance, even if there really is more than one chance. If they did not take the opportunity seriously, don't give a second or third chance easily.

This applies not only to opportunities to obtain or experience something new. It also applies to what a person already has.

Use wisely.

In a culture so rich with options and resources, in a culture always looking forward to the "new and improved," it is easy to become careless and fail to preserve and protect what we already have.

Being resourceful is a matter of using all your resources as fully and creatively as possible. When things can be so easily discarded and replaced, the motivation to value our resources is lowered.

The best antidote for this problem is to restore the missing ingredients of some age-old parental mantras. You may recognize some of these as if I just turned on a tape recording of your father's voice. If not, I recommend you familiarize yourself with each one enough to make a tape of your own voice in your child's mind.

Did you ever hear this one? *Don't walk across people's lawns.* The idea behind this commandment was to respect other people's property. Whatever belongs to other people should be protected and cared for. If you have to go to the front door, stay on the sidewalk.

How about this one? *Return what you borrow in better condition than you borrowed it.* Here again the idea is that being given the use of someone else's possession was an act of trust on their part. You should honor that privilege by paying them back with some kind of acknowledgement that shows you recognize the value of what you borrowed. If you borrowed a car, bring it back washed. If you borrowed a paintbrush, clean it up real good.

Here's another golden oldie. *If you can't take care of this, I will take it away.* And the second one is like it: *You'd better take care of that one, because it is the last one you're going to get.* Of course, the only value in giving warnings of this sort is in the follow-through. Kids are frequently careless with their toys and possessions. After the second time a child leaves his bike out in the rain it should be put up for a week. Not after the fourth or fifth time.

And here's another echo from the past. *We're not going to just run right out and get another one. You're going to have to see if you can figure out how to fix his one.* Obviously, this is something you say to older children who have the knowledge and ability to try to fix something. The point is to challenge them to try. More is learned in trying to fix things than simply to replace them. This is true not only when it comes to resources but also to relationships. You'll be teaching one of life's most valuable lessons if you urge your children to push toward solving problems rather than just discarding them.

These and many other similar statements should play repeatedly in your home. However, as the old saying goes, much more is caught than taught. Parents have many excellent opportunities to teach resourcefulness by their example.

You'll be teaching one of life's most valuable lessons if you urge your children to push toward solving problems rather than just discarding them.

Whether or not you are already in the habit of regular oil changes or keeping your car washed, this is a routine you can always involve the kids in. Ask them to go along with you every time you go do these chores.

Do you make your bed? Do you shine your shoes? The kids need to see you taking care of everyday possessions. After you mow, sweep the sidewalk. Brush the grass off the mower before you put it up. Your kids will notice.

When the hair blower goes dead, even if you don't know the first thing about appliances, don't just throw it away. Bring it out to the kitchen table and let your kids see you at least trying to take it apart enough to clean the lint out of the wire mesh where it sucks in air. This might actually fix the problem (it has for me a few times) which will impress your kids. But even if you can't fix it, your kids will see you try, and that is the lesson in itself.

Another big opportunity you have occurs during occasions like Halloween or school projects. Rather than running out to buy pre-made costumes or doing the same-old, same-old science projects that all the other kids are doing, try working with materials you already have around the house.

As you can see, teaching resourcefulness requires an investment of time on your part. Once again, we are faced with the sobering fact about the art of homemade character. You can't pass on what you don't have.

Now is a good time to renew your commitment to

mix these missing ingredients into your life as well as your kids. We've looked at seven of these missing ingredients that used to be part of a culture that produced people of better character: chores, pain, the woodshed, ma'am, black and white TV, cold peas, and hand me downs. Each of these is like the parts of a cookie recipe that are not tasty by themselves: oil, flour, baking soda, vanilla extract, and salt. Now we turn to three final icons that are more pleasant, like the sweet things we nibble on even before the cookies are baked.

RECIPE STEPS:
HAND-ME-DOWNS

- ◼ Don't overlook the importance of resourcefulness that ranks up there with the more popular traits such as honesty and respect.

- ◼ Encourage people to choose wisely and work effectively the first time by not always giving second and third chances to get something right.

- ◼ Break the habit of giving multiple reminders.

- ◼ Don't be afraid to use the consequence of forfeiture.

- ◼ Take care of your possessions and property, as well as that of others.

- ◼ Try to fix what breaks before you throw it out.

- ◼ How can you create homemade character if everything else you do or use is pre-made or pre-assembled rather than homemade?

Chapter Nine

Table Talk

I remember when the first McDonalds came to Syracuse. Then everything changed. Before McDonalds we used to eat out maybe once a month. When we travelled, we packed lunches and suppers and pulled off the road into a rest area and asked, "Who has the tuna fish? Who has peanut butter and jelly?" as we handed out slightly flattened sandwiches.

The fast food descendants of patriarchal McDonalds almost single-handedly destroyed the American family supper table. By the mid 1990s it was not uncommon for a student to go home for the holidays from the boarding school I led and eat less than two meals at home during the three week break.

I'm not decrying the fact of the fast food takeover of the family lifestyle, but I am bemoaning the worse casualty of all.

Table talk.

Sitting around the supper table I learned to think, to accept criticism, to give an account of my day. The five of us made our entries into a verbal diary for which supper time held the key. We challenged each other's attitudes, exposed each other's pettiness, tried cases, pronounced verdicts, formulated opinions, pursued trivia, learned conversational protocol, sharpened wits, jockeyed for position, all between bites of slowly eaten food.

If someone's day spilled over into a bad mood, it was quickly sponged up with the towel of talk. If the President of the United States had made a foreign policy decision, we became kitchen cabinet advisors. Table talk is where we found words for our beliefs and learned to support them with proofs. Although it can never be proven, my theory is that my IQ grew through table talk. At the table I learned to think, learned to joke, learned to organize my sentences, and learned to project my voice.

> **Sitting around the supper table I learned to think, to accept criticism, to give an account of my day.**

At the table I was confronted with the reality of my true self. I was a stubborn, hard-to-reason-with, know-it-all. The haunting words of my Dad, "You can't tell Doug anything," spoken in almost daily frustration at the supper table eventually prodded me into becoming a good listener today. This boy who once had to make his point now tries to lean forward to catch every word from someone else's mind. All of this happened because of table talk.

My mom is a strong person, but it was during table talk one night that I learned how strong people can be unexpectedly fragile just beneath the surface. I don't remember the topic of discussion. I just remember we were locked in fervent conversation when suddenly my mother burst into tears, pushed her chair back from the table, and left crying in the direction of the bedroom. I was stunned. The discussion stopped instantly. We hadn't been talking about her or against her, so what was she upset about? To this day I don't know. And she never did anything like that again. But that one incident taught me to be careful with people, because they usually have an underground river of emotions and unfinished business just below the surface. I learned that during table talk.

The family supper time is a missing ingredient that leaves us without the immense character development benefits of table talk. Let's look at those benefits in detail, so we can know what to bring back even if the family supper table is an antique.

Accountability

It was at the daily table that I learned the two-pronged role of accountability, for it provided both the bright light of examination and the ominous cloud of foreboding. Both of these painful benefits of account-ability provide power for character development.

The bright light of examination. Our times around the kitchen table were reminiscent of the now defunct "class meetings" of the historic Methodist movements in England and America during which attendees were examined point blank with salient life-questions such as, "How goes it with your soul?" It was at the table where important "follow-up questions" were asked, such as, *How goes it with your math homework? Did you get your chores done? What are your plans? Did you follow through on your word?*

At the table I was examined to see whether my performance matched my abilities. And when my per-formance did not make the ability-appropriate grade, it was here I faced the question, "Why not?" with either words or awkward silence.

The ominous cloud of foreboding. Table talk around an evening meal together was as certain as the setting sun. So I could count on having to give an account for my day. Sometimes, maybe even many times, the search-light never fell on me. But the mere fact that I knew it was possible created a healthy incentive to stick to my work, my words *and* my worth. You see, accountability —no matter how intrusive it may feel—says you count.

No doubt, my work mattered to my folks and so did my words. By holding me accountable they communicated a sense of dignity to me. They were not holding me to their standards. They were shaping in me my own. Standards that told me what I was capable of believing and achieving.

Criticism and Clear Thinking

The day my mom ran crying from the table—if I had to hazard a guess—I'd say she had had it up to the graying tip of her top hair with "all the arguing."

As the only woman in a household of four males, she probably did not intuitively appreciate the sport of it all. The verbal jousting. The sheer thrill of throwing your opponent to the mat using the forward momentum of his poorly chosen words.

I'm sure there were many evenings when I didn't taste one bite of my salmon patties due to the vigorous debate being waged at my opponent's one-yard line. There were plenty of times I tried four times to push my point into the end zone, but failed to score. Usually because my older brother could close the gap in my weak logic.

In these times of table talk I experienced more defeat, more blunt criticism than I ever experienced in actual sports. And for the most part I learned to handle it. Even when I didn't handle it well, I knew it, and I knew what handling criticism should feel like.

Character development requires fearless honesty, thorough reflection and self-examination. But no person ever learns self-examination without significant others showing how to do it and where to look through non-destructive criticism.

Notice I did not use the clichéd term "constructive criticism." The reason is because the kind of criticism we need in character development is not cushioned criticism, which is how we typically understand constructive criticism. On the contrary, all non-destructive criticism is ultimately constructive whether it comes across like it at the time.

Encouragement

Character development requires the oxygen of hope, encouragement and grace. We'll look more closely at this principle in the final chapter called, "Vick's Vaporub."

Paradoxically, it is in the heated environment of table talk that encouragement takes place most powerfully. I have found a truism in life: *the most trustworthy words of encouragement come from a person who will also take you to task about your errors and weaknesses.*

The irony is this: if all you ever offer me are compliments, I find it increasingly difficult to believe them. Over time, since I know myself all too well, I find it incredible that someone would never notice my weaknesses, become annoyed, and call them to my attention. I subconsciously suspect that I am the subject of mere flattery.

Flattery is the fools gold of encouragement. It only appears to offer something valuable. Even parents, not just politicians, can try to use flattery to gain something. Just because the goal is good – namely, building Johnny's self-esteem – doesn't mean flattery is good.

Encouraging words register in the heart of the hearer only when they come with the stereo channel of sincere critique. The fact that table talk can be so blunt and animated, so challenging and merciless, is the very reason that any compliment in that context enjoys resonance and resilience in a person's sense of worth.

The most trustworthy words of encouragement come from a person who will also take you to task about your errors and weaknesses.

Suffice it to say that nothing could be better to make those precious words of encouragement ring true than the realm of table talk.

The Relentless "How"

It was during table talk where I learned to turn pipe dreams into practical plans or toss them out. Because it was there that I faced what I have come to call the relentless "how." Here's how it works:

Suppose as a junior higher I came to the table with a big idea to go solo backpacking. I announce the idea with my characteristic truimphalism, as if the challenge has already been met by the mere announcement itself. Mind you, it matters not that I had never once gone camping, or even made it through the night in the pup tent set up in the backyard!

This is a fact my older brother is more than happy to point out ungraciously, "How do you plan to do that? Hold it all night? Or keep an empty mayonnaise jar in the tent?" And thus comes the first *how* thrust in my face.

Regardless of the sneering tone with which it is delivered, it is a reasonable question which calls for a plan of action. "I'll bring a flashlight, so I won't be scared of the dark when I go outside to... you know." (We weren't allowed to say words like... well, you know.)

"Actually, come to think of it," Rick adds on a roll now, "you might not have to go outside the tent in the middle of the night anyways, because you probably will never get in it in the first place. How are you going to set up the tent by yourself?" There is the second *how*.

I counter, "I can practice here at home before I go."

"Great! Good plan. Let's see... what else are you going to have to practice? Oh, who knows. Maybe making a campfire, cooking over it, digging a latrine, not whining when you hear scary animal sounds at night! How are you going to find time to practice all those things?"

The third *how*. But now I'm moving with the rhythm of it. "I don't know, but you can help me train by being the skunk. You're a natural!" Vainly, I imagine that I just scored a point. As usual, my older brother never gives me the satisfaction of an acknowledged touché.

At this point, also as usual, my parents jump in with much less sarcasm to keep the relentless how's from piling up too furiously.

"How are you planning to get there?"

"How will you get word to us if you need help?"

"How are you going to pay for the equipment you'll need? All we have is the pup tent."

On and on they come. *How's* to the left of me. *How's* to the right of me.

Maybe this is why I had an affinity for playing the goalie position in high school and college sports. I came to enjoy trying to snag every *how* that was shot in my direction.

In the process, I learned strategic thinking: how to clarify goals, how to identify objectives, how to prioritize outcomes, and how to enumerate my tactics. And in the process I ultimately learned what kind of things were worth the effort of facing the relentless how.

This was great training. Even though moral character is mostly a matter of the will, sound thinking about goals, values and objectives inform and sustain the will in its quest for determination.

For anyone to gain moral clarity and strength he or she must inculcate this habit of facing the relentless how. Living a life of character begins within an initial how question in almost every circumstance. How do I plan to remain honest in the face of the urge to self-protection? How will I keep my promise even when I feel too tired at the end of the day? How will I plan to sustain a grateful attitude even if this physical infirmity persists? These are all first stage questions. But to succeed in living life with sound character, each of these questions require a second, third and fourth follow-up how or we won't persevere in our intentions.

The habit of asking the relentless how is best developed with the help of unrelenting, but ultimately loving interrogators who do the asking for us until we learn how. Table talk is the place where this can happen daily.

There will be no character development without the elements of table talk. If our cultural lifestyle has so persecuted the family resulting in a modern diaspora, a scattering of family members to the distant shores of mall, ball practice, and church meetings, and if the result is the loss of table talk, a way must be found to place the components of table talk back into the lives of our children. But I dare say, even if those ways are found there will always be something less satisfying than was found around the supper table. Like mashed potatoes without butter.

$\mathcal{R}$ECIPE $\mathcal{S}$TEPS: *TABLE TALK*

- ▣ Make one meal a day with your family all together a top priority.
- ▣ Make sure that mealtime is suited for conversation.
  - *At least a half hour.*
  - *Turn off the TV.*
  - *No earphones.*
  - *No newspapers.*
- ▣ Referee the conversation in order to let everyone speak. But don't call too many fouls. Good table talk like good sports requires a referee who can say, "Play on."
- ▣ Bring a set of routine accountability questions to the table nearly every day.
- ▣ When things are said that are "off the wall" or "illogical" wait to see if the group process results in correction. You don't have to fix every comment.
- ▣ Make sure the conversation is sprinkled with encouraging and positive words. But don't worry about doing it too much. A little salt goes a long way.
- ▣ When someone makes a statement of intention or commitment, practice asking "how" until no one can think of any more to ask on the subject. Make a game out of it from time to time.

123

Chapter Ten

Helping Dad

I was crawling on my belly between the rafters and the roof of the back porch my Dad had decided to remodel and weatherproof. My job was to roll out and staple the insulation. I was about eleven, still under five feet tall and less than a hundred pounds. That's why I was the one in the tight spot crawling on my belly... well... that and the apparently unalterable fact of my father's, shall we say, girth.

I remember being hot and sweaty, my exposed skin acting like a Petri dish for growing deadly colonies of itches from the spores of fiberglass insulation I was breathing and accumulating. Like undergoing Chinese water torture, I was being driven insane by the prickles. But I didn't mind, because I was helping Dad.

That was an unusual situation when I actually got to do something. Most of my growing up years were spent in the state of suspended animation, while holding the flashlight on whatever screw Dad was tightening. For the first few years of my life I don't recall any real true conversations between me and Dad. "Come here and hold this," was my invitation to a relationship. "Hold the light still," was the extent of his expectations for that relationship. Sometimes holding still seemed as unbearable as eating insulation particles. But usually I didn't mind, because I was helping Dad.

As I grew older the form of our relationship became a source of frustration for me. When would I get to use the hammer, wield a paint brush, and start the chain saw? After all, by this time my younger brother Steve was tall enough to hold the light. I felt like I was being held back in school. I would complain, Dad would relent, and I would enjoy a brief moment of inexplicable delight of pounding the nail while he watched.

Invariably, the nail bent. Or when I finally progressed to the stage where I could drive a nail straight down without folding it over, I would strike the last blow just a little too hard and leave a crescent shaped depression in the wood. Dad would point out the mistake, even if he hadn't been in the room at the time.

It was as if he could be anywhere on earth and, if I did it wrong, whatever "it" might happen to be, Dad would pause, cock his head in the direction of the source of imbalance in the world of perfect workmanship, and drop whatever he was doing to fly to the scene instantly like Superman. He had an eagle eye for detail and could detect and swoop down on an unsmoothed rough spot, an unwashed fleck of dirt, and anything uncentered or unleveled.

By the time I hit my teen years, I no longer enjoyed working with Dad or even for Dad, no matter how much I got paid for things like washing the car. His standards were too high. Maybe he liked spending his whole life getting every last little bug off the chrome bumper of our 1967 Impala, but I had a motorcycle in the garage that begged for my attention. A once over on the chrome would have to do, and I was off on my 160cc chopped down Harley dirtbike. But no matter how fast I took the jumps, nor how long I stayed out in the fields, nor how loud I revved the engine I could not muffle the worry that Dad would be home soon, notice the bugs, and say, "You missed a few spots."

By now the word "perfectionist" is focusing in your mind. My Dad is such a perfectionist he had his own language that would come out anytime things were getting messed up. We had to be careful not to *squudgen up* anything textile, like bedspreads or pressed clothing. If we weren't careful we might *bollix up* anything that had to be arranged in proper order, like his evenly stacked coins on the bureau. Even substantial solid objects like furniture could be *rimracked* and somehow spoiled.

Unfortunately, perfectionism has gotten a lot of bad press recently. It is reviled as a form of child abuse.

"P" is the new scarlet letter, replacing Hester Prynne's "A". And yes, go ahead and plaster the letter all over my Dad; he is a perfectionist. But I'm glad. I wouldn't trade my years of helping Dad for anything less. His standards were high. But that was only because something is either clean or it is not. Something is either straight or it is not. Something is either finished or it is not.

All those years of watching my Dad taught me the one constant in life that is the bedrock of character: things need to be done right. It is THE standard. Settling for anything less falls short. I don't know why this standard is so destructive to some people but wasn't to me. I'm sure part of the reason had to do with the way my Dad exulted in a job well done. Striving for excellence was joy, because it was not an illusive and unapproachable standard. It was earthy. Tactile.

> **Something is either clean or it is not. Something is either straight or it is not. Something is either finished or it is not.**

My Dad loves excellence so much that he would come all the way up from the basement with a piece of wood in his hand, interrupt whatever anyone was doing, and invite us to "Feel this!" as if he had just found the Hope Diamond in an old suitcase in our crawl space. It wasn't just a piece of maple that he had spent an hour sanding to blonde perfection. He had emerged from Plato's shadowy cave with the real Form in his hands. True Smoothness. He would take our hands in his dusty fingers and help us touch smoothness with almost uncomfortable passion.

We didn't realize at the time that the same thing was happening to us as the wood. We were being shaped by his consistent movements stroking across our minds the standard of excellence. All those years of holding the light and watching Dad work, created a stage on which one actor had performed the role of craftsman, reciting the one line soliloquy, "Things need to be done right."

> **Like anything powerful, the standard of excellence is dangerous if not handled carefully.**

There will be no character development without this ingredient of helping Dad—some adult who models excellence and holds young people to some measure of accountability. Like anything powerful, the standard of excellence is dangerous if not handled carefully.

Acceptance.

The problem with establishing high standards is what to do when people do not reach, or measure up to, those standards. What do you say to a five year old who brings you a drawing of a horse that looks like the Goodyear blimp with legs and a tail? Should you say it is good when it is not? Everybody is familiar with those young bubbly parents who think the world is one great big refrigerator door for displaying every single masterpiece of their child's superlative talent—the kind who videotape every burp and gurgle as if the child should win the Nobel prize for existence. Gag.

On the other hand you don't want to hold the horse picture in one hand, set Billy on your knee, and begin to critique his drawing for composition, form, and color. Emily Dickinson would remind us that there are times to:

> *Tell the truth but tell it slant, success in cir-*
> *cuit lies.*

Somehow you have to walk that tight wire between true evaluation and loving acceptance. How do you do that?

First, you don't have to praise the object at all. You can praise the level of effort put forward. You don't need to say, "My that is a wonderful horse!" Instead you should comment or ask a question about the level of effort the drawing involved.

Many times children will present their drawings like toddlers play the "drop game." That's the game where Billy drops his fork on the floor, watches Mommy pick it up, and has the clever idea of dropping it again. Mommy picks it up again, and Billy enjoys his first experience as a puppeteer with Mommy jerking around on the end of strings he manipulates.

In the same way, Billy can draw a horsey, bring it to Mommy, get a hug and kiss, watch her stick it on the refrigerator and repeat the process endlessly with nothing more than scribbles on paper.

It is not hard to avoid this trap and at the same time teach a basic principle about excellence. Since excellence takes time and effort, teach Billy to evaluate his own products from the standpoint of effort. If the drawing shows effort you can say, "This looks like you spent a lot of time and thought of everything. You remembered that a horse has four legs, a tail, a head, and a mane. Good thinking."

In this way you are teaching that acceptance is not based on the quality of the final product but on the quality of the person. A person who is lazy and does not try is not behaving in an acceptable way. But a person who tries hard is, no matter what the quality of the resulting product.

However, we don't want to make it seem as if the quality of the final product is unimportant. You are not going to read this book and evaluate my writing based on how much effort I put into it. Don't we also want to teach lessons about excellent achievement as well as excellent effort? After all, when Billy gets into school he will inevitably encounter one of those old-fashioned teachers who still believe that an "A" is given to an essay only if it is an "A" essay, regardless if the author gave "A" effort. That's real life. So how can you help Billy learn to discern true excellence without crushing his spirit or damaging his self esteem?

Let's get one thing straight about self-esteem. Built on anything but the truth, self-esteem is worthless.

Many psychologists teach that normal people have an aversion to believing good things about themselves if they know those things to be false. That is a lesson too sparsely applied to issues of building children's self-esteem. You get nothing of value out of merely attempting to make a child feel good about himself.

True unshakable self-esteem can occur only in a person who lives, thinks, and acts in valuable ways. So paradoxically, people with higher self-esteem will be the result of techniques for building self-esteem that employ truth and honest criticism.

How can I ever believe your compliments if I am not sure you are willing to criticize? There is actually more security for a child who hears occasionally, "This is not very good." If compliments aren't dispensed like gum balls, they will be a more meaningful and effective treat when they come.

One of the most effective things you can do to help establish a young person's critical acumen is to solicit his involvement in the process of judging his own work. Simply put—don't evaluate one drawing (or whatever it may be) at a time. Always look for a point of comparison, and ask him "How does this compare with the last picture you did? Which do you think is better? Why?"

If you have no previous drawing for comparison, say, "Thank you, but I want to wait to talk about it or hang it up until you do another picture sometime." At that later time, have her choose which she thinks is better. Don't just keep hanging pictures up on the refrigerator. Require her to select one or two that she thinks is best. Always have her identify, why she thinks it is superior.

You can do this with everything. "Do you think you did a better job washing the car this time or last time?" These kinds of comparative questions open the door for the parent's input about what was good and what could have been better.

By taking this approach you are teaching two very important things. First, you are teaching her to become comfortable with self evaluation and self criticism, which will shape her into a less defensive person. Second, you are exposing her to the thought patterns in the world of excellence. All the while you are not jeopardizing her sense of acceptance.

Accessibility

Another problem with holding up standards of excellence is the way they can seem out of reach to young people who have previously not excelled in the areas that the world tends to reward. It is disheartening watching friends get straight "A's", making the varsity football team, or achieving first chair in the clarinet section and never finding yourself on the top of the achievement scale. It is so disheartening that early on in life many kids give up the attitude of striving, because it gets them nowhere.

A quick look back a hundred years ago and the solution to this problem can be easily seen. Where was television? Did children have access to information about the best of the best? No. They were not afflicted with the mental illness brought on by images of superstardom. Their world of examples was smaller. Standards of excellence were smelled at county fair pie contests; they were heard in the accurate spelling of *onomatopoeia* in the annual spelling bee. There was no national and international media bringing superstars into our living room day in and day out elevating the standard of excellence into an unreachable ionosphere.

> A quick look back a hundred years ago... There was no national and international media bringing superstars into our living room day in and day out elevating the standard of excellence into an unreachable ionosphere.

In order to strive for chess playing excellence children did not have to compare themselves with Bobby Fisher. Excellence was closer to home. It was not way off in New York City or Paris. Excellence could be found in the toolshed where Dad was repairing a chair leg. It was on the living room couch where Mom was nightly tethered to ball of yarn knitting a star pattern afghan.

If we are to help our young people strive for excellence we must close the distance between them and the vision of the goal. We must first deflate the unreal standards of excellence floating through the airwaves into our homes. Teach children that the world tends to prize achievements that don't matter. Turn off the *Oscar's*. Turn off the *Miss America Pageant*. Or at least let them hear you say, "These people are good at what they do, but what they do is relatively insignificant. Imagine all the normal things they have neglected in order to be where they are."

Tell them that it is much more valuable to pursue excellence without neglecting normal life and relationship like the little thirteen year old superstar gymnasts do in order to be fitted with their brief moment of golden glory. You need to work as aggressively to separate children from the brainwashing of modern celebrity worship as cult watchers work to rescue and deprogram brainwashed devotees of Sun Myung Moon.

Point them in the direction of the things worth their best effort. Work at honest, caring relationships. Involve yourself in local improvements. Challenge yourself never to hold an opinion that you can't support with facts. By doing so you will be giving the inestimable gift of bringing the goal of excellence back within reach.

Stop and think about it. The pursuit of moral excellence is perhaps the one pursuit where everyone is on a

135

> **The pursuit of moral excellence is perhaps the one pursuit where everyone is on a level playing field.**

level playing field. It does not require superb physical prowess or intellectual ability provided by genetic inheritance. It does not require academic or economic advantages provided by family income. A poor person can scrub a floor as spotlessly clean as a rich person. A "D" student can miter a piece of cove molding as precisely as a genius. An uncoordinated egghead can bake a fluffy meringue to perfection as easily as an Olympic gold medalist.

There are no barriers to the pursuit of excellence once a person simply decides to pursue it. Plus, there are good examples all around in every social class, racial group, and economic strata. Kids just have to be taught to "keep your eyes peeled," as my Dad used to say.

The only thing that varies from person to person is the amount of encouragement they receive along the way. Unfortunately, too many children do not get very much encouragement from the people closest to them. This, however, is not a serious barrier or even a necessary ingredient. History is full of stories of people whose inspiration and encouragement came from adults outside their home and family.

Once awakened the passion for excellence is so strong that the human heart will attach itself wherever examples are found. The trick is waking up this passion. How is that done?

Accountability.

Perhaps there is no greater gift you can give a young person than to expect of him or her moral excellence.

During a three year stint as a church youth director I rejected the "in vogue" methodologies of *motivation by engourgement*: pizza bashes, weekend frenzies, and Christian music festivals. I believed, instead, that young people will tend to rise to the level of expectations if they are given good reasons.

For three years I planned weekend events with such attractive purposes as memorizing scripture for two solid days, engaging in a thirty-hour book study on a regular schoolyear weekend, or undergoing a three-day *Old-Fashioned Thanksgiving Retreat*. On this occasion teenagers were invited to fast for two days and required to sleep in cabins without heat (in late November on the shore of Lake Ontario) and work outside all day long. The amazing thing is that they loved those events. There were students ranging from valedictorians to dropouts. Everyone memorized. Everyone read and discussed. Everyone worked. These events profoundly influenced their lives permanently.

One girl, Tracy, came on the Old- Fashioned Thanksgiving retreat. Even at the young age of seventeen, she was twisted by the emotional and physical effects of drugs and sexual promiscuity. During that weekend I spoke with her only once. Conversation was not a focus for the event. Journaling was. So the weekend was relatively quiet. Even if that weren't the case, I'm not sure I would have known much about what was going on inside of Tracy. She didn't talk often around this group of kids who weren't like her friends at school.

A week after the retreat, Tracy was sitting in the dentist chair having a routine tooth extraction when she died. She was over-anesthetized. The family's devastation was somewhat relieved when Tracy's journal from the retreat was found in her Bible. The halting words gave clear expression to a passion that had been lit in her heart for moral excellence, even though it would require a cessation of an entire lifestyle of drugs and sex. I never forgot that lesson of how young people don't need to be talked at, or preached to. Put them in situations where a great deal is being expected of them and a sleeping passion is awakened.

How do you properly expect so much out of young people? We have already talked about stretching kids through the use of chores in chapter two. Beyond that you need to become comfortable with these words, "Go back and do it again." When you know that a young person could have done better and had the time to do so, it is right to let him know when his efforts or product is not acceptable.

I can hardly write these words without feeling defensive, as I imagine scores of readers thinking I am being hard-nosed and insensitive. After all, we are living in a world where some popular educational theories question why a child should have to spell words a particular way. "That's too rigid. Why not let them come up with their own creative way of spelling? After all we don't want to stifle them or discourage them."

It is in the face of the spirit of an age that has produced such theoretical drivel that I have the nerve to suggest that we should tell a kid to go back and do it over, if it is not good enough. I do it unapologetically.

The things I have excelled in, like clarinet or piano or soccer or lacrosse, I excelled in because someone was there telling me, "You didn't practice long enough; you'll have to do the same lesson again this week." We need to fearlessly apply the same technique to other expectations we have of our children. "I'm sorry that's not thorough enough; you'll have to do it again. That's not respectful enough; you'll have to say it again."

Invariably, Dad always came home from work. I had gotten off the motorcycle and was ready for my five dollars for washing the car. But there was no five dollars. Not yet. First we went on a stroll together. Bonding time. Dad led me out to the driveway where we walked around the car and spotted what I had missed. "You need to go back and take care of those." I nodded. Unthrilled.

That was then. This is now. I wouldn't trade one moment of holding the flashlight or spotting missed bugs on chrome bumpers. This unwanted accountability, this love-hate relationship with his standards and expectations awoke my passion for excellence. My life is smoother because of his dusty fingers and consistent passion for things being right. If it weren't for helping Dad, I wouldn't be writing this book.

ℛECIPE Ŝ TEPS: *HELPING DAD*

- ▣ Teach the pursuit of excellence in the things that really matter.
- ▣ Live by this motto which is the bedrock of character: *things need to be done right.* Teach it unceasingly by word and by example.
- ▣ Avoid damaging "perfectionism" as you hold up the standards of excellence by learning how to communicate acceptance even when performance is not acceptable.
  - *It is right to let a person know when his efforts or product is not acceptable.*
  - *Solicit his involvement in the process of judging his own work.*
  - *Ask comparative questions which open the door for the parent's input about what was good and what could have been better.*
  - *Teach her to become comfortable with self evaluation and self criticism, which will shape her into a less defensive person.*
- ▣ Avoid damaging "perfectionism" as you hold up the standards of excellence by showing how accessible excellence is to any person.
  - *Close the distance between a person and the vision of the goal.*

- *Deflate the unreal standards of excellence floating through the airwaves into our homes.*
- *Expose the error that the world tends to prize achievements that don't matter.*
- *Inspire people with the fact that moral excellence is perhaps the one pursuit where everyone is on a level playing field.*
- *Point them in the direction of the things worth their best effort.*

▣ **Avoid damaging "perfectionism" as you hold up the standards of excellence through the wise use of accountability.**

- *Become comfortable with these words, "Go back and do it again" when you know that a person could have done better and had the time to do so.*
- *Awaken the passion for excellence through a consistent expectation for things being right.*

Chapter Eleven

Vick's Vaporub

I might as well come clean, finally, at the last chapter of a book on homemade character. From an early age my character has often been suspect. And rightly so.

For example, even though I never kept a written log, I dare say that half of the time I stayed home from school due to sickness, I was faking.

I also dare say Mom knew each time.

What always left me unsettled was that I never knew when Mom knew. Try as I might, scanning her voice patterns, feeling the subtle nuances of her touch, I could not detect any difference in her bedside manner between those times I was faking and the times I really was sick.

To this day I have a highly developed sixth sense more sophisticated than the most sensitive lie detectors. This comes from years of trying to read into my Mom's mannerisms. Ask my wife who has been too often the unhappy subject of these delicately honed skills, too often unable to escape the obsequious readings triggered by my insecurities.

Why was Mom so inscrutable?

I am convinced it was because she was so steady. She had a way of coming into my room and sitting on the bed beside my sickness always the same way. Whether or not I had a chest cold, it was like she always brought the soothing aroma of *Vick's Vaporub.*

Vick's was the world's cure for the common cold. Perhaps it had no medicinal value. But its penetrating vapors brought the smell of being loved to young girls and boys like me who were either sick or simply scared of school that day.

And Mom knew. And understood.

She never once said, "I don't believe you're sick. Prove it."

Perhaps this was because she lived her life at the edge of fatigue with self-disappointing desires to have her struggle to be a good mom—and how hard it was —understood. I don't know. As an adult I have come to recognize those feelings. And I can now imagine that it wasn't hard for her to understand that sometimes things just feel hard, and a young kid simply needs somebody to say, "That's OK. Today you can just lie there and not face the tests."

Perhaps slowly circling fingertips rubbing *Vick's*

Vaporub on a boy's chest brought as much relief to her as to me, relief for its utter simplicity. There were no complicated questions about it, no uncertainties about discipline, or decisions, or advice, or worries. No unwanted feelings of self-pity midst unending loads of laundry and stacks of dishes. No "how am I going to get all this done" pressures.

It was simple "mothering." This moment grounded her. It meant home for her as much as for me.

Vick's Vaporub. It represents understanding, grace, comfort and personal care which must fill the atmosphere of any home wherever the hard challenges of character development are being issued.

I was undoubtedly a weak, struggling, conniving, cheating, disrespectful, complaining young boy much of the time, but the aroma of understanding and patience never left our home because Mom was always there, unflappably present, believing I was worth loving, making me feel like I was easy to love. Even when one day my underwear was discovered at the top of a pine tree. Which is another story for another time, though to this day I cannot for the life of me remember any satisfactory explanation.

Vick's Vaporub. Unfortunately, there are signs that this icon of mothercare is fading like a swirling whisp of fragrance.

Now before I go any farther let me say unequivocally that what follows is not intended to judge or induce a guilt trip. However, we need to recognize how our culture makes the most penetrating elements of mothering less present or at least less pungent. It's true that moms will always be moms. But there is a risk that mothercare is devolving into something less conducive to character development? Something less penetratingly present? Something less *Vick's*?

Chauffeur Moms

Kids need to see their parents' faces, not just the back of their heads as they are being chauffeured from activity to activity. Parenting does not happen well from the driver's seat.

Everyone knows you can't carry on a satisfying conversation when the other person's head is buried in the newspaper. Just as true, you can't connect with children when your head is buried in busy city or mental traffic.

If it feels like you're always in drive and seldom in park with your family, only you can shift gears. But shift gears you must.

Your home must be characterized by plenty of time when people are just around, not running around. One of the greatest enemies in this regard is a parent's tendency to

> **Fifty years ago, before organized sports, dance lessons, and gymnastic classes, parents were not afraid to shove kids out the front door into the world of "nothing to do."**

be held hostage by the fear of kids being "bored."

Fifty years ago, before organized sports, dance lessons, and gymnastic classes, parents were not afraid to shove kids out the front door into the world of "nothing to do."

"Nothing to do?" they'd say unsympathetically. "Go find something." It's your problem. Fend for yourself.

It is not a parent's job to be cruise director on the good ship *S.S. Funtime*.

When you stop spending so much time exporting the kids in the minivan to distant venues of fun, you're around home more. There wonderful scenarios can be created by a bold conviction to force kids to make their own fun. And you'll enjoy the casual crisscrossings where family members intersect, like the following:

Billy bursts through the kitchen door, a cloud of dusty dirt swirls in the wake of his breathless excitement, "Mom, there's this huge frog out by the big pine tree! Can I catch it and bring it in?"

"Whoa mister! Slow down. What are you gonna catch it in?"

"Nothing. I'm gonna use my bare hands. I'm not scared."

"You may not be, but who says I want a frog in the house?"

"Are you scared of a frog, Mom?"

"Depends on how good a grip you have on him."

147

"I won't let him get away. Promise."

"That may be a harder promise to keep than you think. Frogs are wiggly."

"I won't let go. Promise."

Mom turns away from the sink, grabs the dishtowel to wipe suds off her hands and closes the deal, "How about I come to the garage and you can show me there."

"Alright! Be right back. I'm not scared. You can touch him, too."

At first glance this episode seems empty of anything profound. But look what just enveloped Billy, like *Vick's Vaporub*. A sense of being listened to, of being bold, of being admired, of being important enough to adjust Mom's agenda.

These are the kinds of *no-account* encounters that happen when people are just *around* rather than always *running around*.

Fast Food Moms

At the risk of sounding sexist, a mom's place of greatest influence is in the kitchen making meals. Of course, in these days of role reversals right and left healthy families can sport a cooking dad instead. Most often, however, the tasks in the kitchen fall to mom. And, as I said, this can be a place of great influence.

However, beware. That influence diminishes when the vital image of servanthood is replaced by the no muss-no fuss culinary art of pulling out microwave dinners and pre-packaged school lunches.

The daily ministrations of making sandwiches and snacks, tearing lettuce and trimming bread crust pump influence and love into the atmosphere as they are repeated rhythmically, like the heartbeat.

Whether we like it or not, we may be wired to feel most loved when food is being provided and prepared for us. Even God Himself, according to Psalm 23, guides us like a shepherd to tasty green pastures and in the end prepares a banquet table for us. Perhaps His most gracious act of self-disclosure may have come during those days when He showered a seed-like substance (called *manna*) from heaven to feed His desert-wandering people with daily bread.

You cannot short-change this divine daily activity of making *manna* happen and still expect to have a home with as much sense of love.

I figured it up. During my 18 growing-up years at home my mom prepared no less than 6300 suppers. I never once felt any sense of her being an unwilling prisoner of the stove and sink. And when each day's meal was ready, she not only called me to supper, but through her faithful display of servanthood, she also called me to a life of character.

Career Moms

My mom's day-in-day-out kitchen service also gave

witness to the fact that she would always be available to help with everything from school projects to memorization tasks.

The first miracle recorded in St. John's gospel tells of the time Jesus of Nazareth turned water into wine. I've always enjoyed how John, who often identified himself as one who was specially loved by Jesus, chose this as his lead off miracle. Not some supernatural act of healing.

Instead, John wanted everyone to see how Jesus —who was about to take twelve followers on a life of extreme character development—demonstrated His readiness to come to the aid of a person who had run out of what it took to fulfill his responsibility as the host of the wedding feast.

This is what kids need to know as well. "I'm ready and available to help, not at my convenience, but at the moment of your need."

This kind of availability is very difficult for moms who work outside the home. Of course I have no right to suggest that all moms should stay home and not have careers. But I cannot gloss over the fact that ample availability is crucial for maintaining an atmosphere that undergirds character development.

Somehow try to seek creative solutions to the challenge of availability. If you must work, is there a way for you to be home at some of the most crucial times of the day? Times like after school, for example.

The value of a parent's presence when a kid comes in the front door is immeasurable. And the value is not always in the opportunity to give a warm embrace or warm cookie.

One day I came home from seventh grade with a cheap ring on my finger. This was a serious oversight, because we were not allowed to wear jewelry. Our church denomination, which since that time has abandoned the jewelry-verboten era for more enlightened times, forbade "superfluous adornment." My dilemma entailed how a young man could declare his undying love for his junior high girlfriend without exchanging "friendship rings."

So I surreptitiously purchased matching rings and secretly entered into schooltime-only betrothal with my love. Each day I would keep the ring in my pocket until I boarded the school bus in the morning, and then slip it off before I came home in the afternoon.

On this occasion, I forgot to take it off.

I didn't notice. But my mom did. I had barely set down my books before she said something. However, she did not go ballistic. She simply asked, "Where'd you get the ring?"

This was one of those times when the *Vick's* gets too strong and makes you choke.

In those simple five words, I heard a life-changing warning: *Doug, don't be two different people. Conniving secrecy is not admirable.*

I'm glad my mom's watchful presence functioned as a loving scanner when I came home from school. There's no telling how much of my character formed while under daily inspection due to her availability.

———————————

Ultimately the special value of Vick's Vaporub had more to do with who was using it. My mom.

Too often sincere and well-meaning efforts at character development either collapse under the burden of unattainable high standards, or veer off course into pompous moralism.

The problem with Browning's famous line, "A man's reach should exceed his grasp" is that we are usually reaching for something high up in a tree at the very tip of the branch. The prospect of failing is almost unavoidable. Consequently, reach should exceed grasp only in the company of a good safety net of grace and forgiveness.

And at the end of the day, that is my mom.

She has always been "for" her family. Though underappreciated and probably amidst untold struggles to keep sacrificing day in and day out, she has been a clear reflection of God's unfailing love. So much so, it really is not too much of a stretch to paraphrase the lyrical biblical text:

If Mom is for us, who can be against us?
She who did not spare her own selfhood but gave

herself up freely for us all, how shall she not also freely give us all she can? And what can separate us from Mom's love?

Let the penetrating aroma of Vick's Vaporub fill your homes. Tender, understanding, unfailing, available love. That's the one ingredient in character development that makes the cookies turn out every time.

$\mathcal{R}$ECIPE $\mathcal{S}$TEPS: *VICK'S VAPORUB*

▣ Character development requires an atmosphere where grace and tenderness are penetratingly present.

▣ Your home must be characterized by plenty of time when people are just *around*, not *running around.*

• *Don't be held hostage by the fear of kids being "bored" which fuels the engines of the on-the-go family.*

• *Stop exporting the kids in the minivan to distant venues of fun.*

• *Force kids to make their own fun and you'll enjoy the casual crisscrossings where family members intersect.*

▣ Make *manna* happen daily. You cannot short-change the daily ministrations of provision and care, like fixing meals, folding clothes, mowing lawns and paying bills, and still expect to have a home with as much sense of love.

▣ Ample availability is crucial for maintaining an atmosphere that undergirds character develop-ment. Seek creative solutions to the challenge of availability.

▣ The value of a dad or mom's presence when a kid comes home from school is immeasurable.